the RESISTANCE

"We may never, this side of death, drive the invader out of our territory, but we must be in the Resistance."

-C.S. Lewis

Response to *The Resistance*

"*The Resistance* will inspire your Jesus-centered faith to the ends of the earth."

—MARK BATTERSON
Lead Pastor, National Community Church
Author of bestselling books including, *The Circle Maker*

"You can't plant what you don't love. Zach Maddox is a church planter and he loves the church. Zach's love for the church shines through in his book. Zach loves a church that is called to conflict, and destined to be glorious. *The Resistance* reminds us of the vibrant, aggressive nature of the church and it will stir in you a passion for the church to rise to the fullness of God's intention. Read *The Resistance* and let it attack the lethargy in your own heart, let the truths therein stir in you a desire to strive for that spotless bride Jesus is coming to claim for Himself. Read *The Resistance* and heed it's call to join in the dance of mission as God glorifies Himself by establishing His church among every people and nation."

—DICK BROGDEN
Strategy Leader, Live | Dead Church Planting Initiative
Middle East/North Africa

"Zach is passionate about God, relationships with people and the Mission of the Church. *The Resistance* is intended to mobilize believers in God's Church to be relentless."

—DR. MIKE RAKES
Lead Pastor, Winston Salem First
Author, *Slings and Stones*

"Zach Maddox takes dead aim at the strategic warfare in which the Church of Jesus is called to engage. It is not always easy. In fact, it is just the opposite. It takes determination and commitment to be identified as a church that truly inspires others to see Jesus. Zach says it well, 'Jesus initiated a revolution. All He wants is a few who will think as He did, love as He did, see as He did, and serve as He did. All He needs is to revolutionize the hearts of a few, and they will impact the world.' A church filled with people like that will be the beginning of The Resistance."

—MARK LEHMANN
Lead Pastor, Cornerstone Church
Bowie, MD

"Zach Maddox has captured the unique place of the church in today's world...a company of believers called out from among the world, separated with a holy calling and mission to reach the world for Christ. As he walks you through the pages of John's Revelation you will discover the church under persecution is always at its best...for Jesus is walking in the midst of the conflict giving orders and encouragement along the way. The Head of the Church is still speaking today. The question is, "Are we listening?" *The Resistance* clearly articulates what the Spirit is saying to the remnant in these final days!"

—ANDY HARRIS
Lead Pastor, The Church of the Cross
Haughton, LA

"No one can write about war better than a soldier whose been in battle. The same things hold true in our spiritual battle. Zach Maddox does not write his thoughts on the battle based on being a casual observer, but as one who lives daily in the midst of it, living in the Middle East. I found Zach's words to be insightful, Biblically grounded, and great guidance for all of us who desire to bring down the enemy of darkness in our lives and world. This book is a winner in every regard!"

—DON JAMES
Lead Pastor, Bethany Church
Wyckoff, NJ

"Zach Maddox in his new book addresses the critical issue of our day. The difference between light and darkness. The church he leads in Jerusalem is uniquely poised under the leading of the Holy Spirit to make an eternal difference in this fiercely contested real estate. The answer will always be the powerful declaration of Gods eternal Word done through the lives of fully devoted followers of Jesus. Zach's book will serve to inspire any reader, but especially those who want to see lasting eternal results for their lives and influence."

—SCOTT ERICKSON
Lead Pastor, Peoples Church
Salem, OR

"In a day and age in which the Church is constantly being redefined, Zach Maddox gives a timeless truth: As Christians we are in a spiritual battle with our adversary - the devil and his cohorts. You will be challenged and encouraged by Zach's call to be "the Church" and resist the Enemy in these perilous times."

—GEORGE FLATTERY
Lead Pastor, Stone Church
Orland Park, IL

"What is the Church of Jesus to be and to do in the days in which we live? In, *The Resistance*, Zach Maddox defines not only the importance of the church, but also its affect on culture and society. If you want to see what the Church is meant to be, this is a must read!"

—JUSTIN LATHROP
Executive Director, Young Pastors

"Zach Maddox delivers a strong message to Christians of this generation. With an engaging blend of past and present voices, *The Resistance* is a timely and powerful reminder to the church to be active and not passive, to advance and not sit as we wait for Jesus' return."

—ELI GAUTREAUX
Chi Alpha Director
Sam Houston State University

the RESISTANCE

THE CHURCH AND ITS MISSION

ZACH MADDOX

The Resistance

Published by Redefining Faith Resources

Details in some anecdotes and stories have been changed to protect the identities of the persons involved.

 The author has added bold and underlined print to Scripture for emphasis.

ISBN: 978-0-9903-9122-7 (print)
ISBN: 978-0-9903-9123-4 (digital)

To my parents Bob and Brenda, for teaching me to love Jesus and His Church.

For my kids, Nate, Haley, and Lucas, may your love for Jesus drive His message in you to the uttermost parts of the world.

CONTENTS

FOREWORD

Any meaningful reading of Scripture clearly leads to this resounding truth: God loves the church! Not only does God love the church, but He has also created humanity to fulfill its intended design in and through the church. The early church father, Cyprian, famously wrote, "No one can have God for his Father who does not have the Church for his mother." What Cyprian knew to be true, too many modern day Christians have forgotten; active involvement in the local church is essential to walking with God and living on mission for God.

It is impossible to live the life that God has called you to live if you are separated from the body of Christ. The Spirit-empowered church is God's plan for bringing redemption to our broken world and, as a pastor, I love seeing the powerful effect the church has on people's lives as they find hope, healing and purpose as a part of the family of God! To that end, I am always encouraged to see a book that boldly calls people to recognize the church's beauty, value and mission. It's my pleasure to recommend Zach Maddox's new book, *The Resistance: The Church and Its Mission.* The pages of this book are saturated with Scripture and filled with insight into how God intends the bride of Christ to work in the world and shape the lives of His people.

What you will find in the chapters that follow is not a call to passive admiration of the church as a religious institution, but an invitation to engage in the church's mission to bring about the transformation individuals and our world desperately needs.

John Lindell
Lead Pastor, James River Church

How to Use This Book

FOR YOU. FOR YOUR SMALL GROUP. FOR YOUR CHURCH.

"Desire that your life count for something great! Long for your life to have eternal significance. Want this! Don't coast through life without a passion."
–John Piper

Church is more than a service. Church is people living life together, helping one another, and serving the world. God's plan is community united in Jesus.

God put together the faith community. The church family of which you are a member is no accident. The friends you make are of God's design. C. S. Lewis in *The Four Loves* relates,

> A secret Master of the Ceremonies has been at work. Christ, who said to the disciples "Ye have not chosen me, but I have chosen you," can truly say to every group of Christian friends, "You have not chosen one another but I have chosen you for one another." The Friendship is not a reward for our discrimination and good taste in finding one another out. It is the instrument by which God reveals to each the beauties of all the others.[1]

Your brothers and sisters in Christ are a part of your life by God's divine appointment. They are there to bring out the best in you and for you to bring out the best in them. He will reveal a greater sense of who you are in Christ by rubbing shoulders with your church family. God dwells in the Church and wants every person to mature in a relational environment. A person may come to Christ alone, but he or she grows in Christ shoulder-to-shoulder.

This book can be read alone, but it was designed with small groups and churches in mind and is best read together. Leaders can use the book trailer under the "media" tab at theresistancemovement.com to generate interest. God wants us to live, serve, and process truth in the context of community.

The purpose of this book is mobilizing the local church to advance the Kingdom of God to the ends of the earth.

The book can be completed as a 12-week study, reading one chapter every week and then responding together through the discussion starters. The final week involves reading the finished faith community letter created from the activities in Chapter 11, celebrating areas where your church excels and finding solutions where improvement is needed. It can also be completed in six weeks, reading two chapters every week and doing the activities of Chapter 11 in the final week together. A concluding video "Called to Conflict" can be found under the "media" tab at theresistancemovement.com to encourage believers to make a commitment to Christ, the Church and the task of storming the gates of hell until His imminent return.

As you work through each chapter, look to change. Following Jesus means being transformed into His image. Each chapter addresses a different quality that will make this a reality. Embrace the message of the book by fulfilling the mission of God on the earth, driving the invader from your territory, and experiencing the blessed and abundant life Jesus promises. Join *The Resistance* by making a commitment to Jesus and the people in His Church. Make your life count for Him in the world!

The Symbol

ישוע (YESHUA)

"If God is for us, who can be against us?"
–Romans 8:31

While researching the content for this book, I visited some local friends at their shop in the Christian Quarter of the Old City (Syriac Exhibition of Silver). They showed me a newly created piece of jewelry. Within the menorah-style lamp stand is embedded the name of Jesus in Hebrew: ישוע (*Yeshua*).

Archeologists have found in the Galilean region many first century lamps made from pottery originating from Jerusalem. They think local residents bought lamps in Jerusalem during annual feasts in order to bring the light of the Temple back to Galilee. Lamps from the Byzantine period have been found with Greek inscriptions that state, "The light of Christ shines for all."

The jewelry refers to John 8 where Jesus declares in the Temple, "I am the light of the world. Whoever follows me will not walk in darkness, but will have the light of life" (v. 12). The light emitting from the lamp forms the letters for Jesus. The church is to reflect this light of Jesus to the world.

The seven-branched menorah design is explained this way: Seven is God's number of completion, but despite the plurality of lamps, it is made of one piece. Seven is one, similar to a rainbow or a week. The presence of the One True God is in the midst of them. In Revelation the lamps represent the Spirit's presence in churches to whom John writes messages from Jesus. Seven churches are listed, yet they are the one bride of Jesus.

jerusalem-christian-jewelry.com

Another aspect of the seven-branch design is that it resembles a tree. In Jewish tradition the menorah is reminiscent of the Tree of Life from the creation story. In the New Testament, Revelation equates the tree with eternal life. Adam and Eve were banished from the tree and Revelation 22 shows those with clean robes have access to it. The menorah speaks of eternal life with God for His bride made available to everyone only through the blood of the Messiah. In John 15, Jesus said, "I am the vine; you are the branches." He is the tree and only in Him can a person live spiritually and produce good fruit.

John records a vision of seven golden lamps with Jesus standing in the midst of them. The seven separate lamp stands represent seven churches located in modern Turkey. They were a light to the world and Jesus, their commander in chief, walked among them.

Jesus is still in the midst of His Church examining, encouraging, and exhorting her to walk in His steps. They are to bring love, justice, and peace (*shalom*) into the world.

This piece of jewelry is a beautiful symbol of the church, symbolizing Jesus' guiding presence in the midst of His people. As His light-bearer, the church is to give hope to every people group in the world. The Savior is leading a movement of believers dedicated to seeing His glory fill the whole earth.

Jesus is in the midst of the Church…leading the Resistance.

Introduction

JESUS LOVES THE CHURCH

"Christ loved the church and gave himself up for her."
–Ephesians 5:25

Within months of my college graduation, I married my college sweetheart, bringing together the North and South. I am from Chicago, and Shellie is from Tennessee/Kentucky. I bought our rings from a jeweler in Chicago, but mine was sized too large. On the wedding day, with Shellie's rings in hand, I anxiously waited at Shellie's house for mine to arrive in the mail. While waiting, I printed wedding programs and took care of last-minute details. The ring arrived. I jumped into my tux and headed to the church for the ceremony.

We were married on July 7 at 7 p.m. Why? Who knows! Guess "7/7 at 7" sounded cool at the time. The music started, people stood, and the doors flew open. There she was, dressed in white, my beautiful bride. As she walked down the aisle to join me at the altar, all kinds of emotions were stirred: joy, fear, excitement, wonder, and love.

The Bible reveals that Jesus is returning for His Bride, the Church. Yet the situation is reversed—the Bride waits at the altar for Jesus to come in all His glory. Paul wrote the church in Ephesus, "Christ loved the church and gave himself up for her, that he might sanctify her, having cleansed her by the washing of water with the word, so that he might present the church to himself in splendor, without spot or wrinkle or any such thing, that she might be holy and without blemish" (Eph. 5:25–27).

What condition will the Church be in when He comes? Will it be holy and without blemish? Will it be living according to His standard?

As a pastor's kid, I grew up in church and came to love the church. She is a clear part of my identity. Not that everyone in the church was always a delight to be around; nonetheless, everyone was family. Just like everyone in your immediate family may not always be a joy to be around, as family, working through problems is a priority to maintain unity and healthy relationships.

Jesus loves the Church; He adores His Bride. She is His priority. He gave His life for her. His followers should love what He loves and make priority what He makes priority. During His earthly ministry, He stated He would establish the Church and entrust her with His message of hope and reconciliation.

People still desire community but are not looking to the local church to address the longing. Some who place faith in Jesus seem content with "me and my Jesus" and prefer to sit on a beach rather than attend a worship gathering. They disregard the importance of engaging in a faith community, a critical part of developing a relationship with God.

Scripture shows the Lord values community as an integral part of faith and a necessary part of spiritual growth. Disregarding the need to engage regularly with fellow believers is to miss the heartbeat of God who resides in perfect community as Father, Son, and Holy Spirit. If God resides in community, surely His creation should as well. The early church models this.

The Apostle Paul, who always had travel companions, wrote liberally about the church. The backbone of this book, however, will focus on what Jesus says.

In the late 1990s, LEGO was in decline. They decided to partner with popular stories like *Star Wars* and *Harry Potter* to generate new interest. Although these partnerships were successful, many other promotional innovations failed. They branched out in several directions, even a television show. The result was continued decline. By 2003 they were still losing money and decided to go "back to the brick." This changed everything. By going back to the brick and limiting innovation, profits climbed and the company stabilized. Instead of LEGO paying royalties, others wished to partner with them. Cash flow trends reversed by going back to the brick and staying true to the original mission. The Church needs to go "back to the brick," the Cornerstone Jesus (Eph. 2:20).

Os Guinness in his book *Renaissance* retells the story of Billy Graham. "Once, after Dr. Billy Graham had returned from preaching in the Soviet Union, he was roundly criticized by a liberal churchman for the simplicity of his message. 'Dr. Graham has set the church back fifty years,' the liberal harmed. Hearing the criticism, Billy answered quietly, 'I wish I could have set the church back two thousand years!'" Guinness goes on to explain that "the gold standard for our faith lies in the past—though not in the first century itself, and not in the early church, but in Jesus himself and the supreme, decisive authority of his lordship, his call and his commands in the Gospels… Thus in this generation as in every generation, we all often go wrong, and it is always time to go back to him in order to go forward and on with God."[1]

Christ loves the Church and His plan for Kingdom advancement is intimately connected to her. The Bride He wants must live according to His plan and purpose. This book is a call for the Church, the Bride of Christ, to develop a lifestyle in anticipation of a heavenly wedding. By doing so, the Church will be best able to globally advance His message.

Jesus directly speaks about the church in Matthew 16 and 18. In Revelation He addresses seven letters to churches in Asia Minor. This book examines the words of Jesus and what He states about His Bride, with the writings of Paul included as supplementary scripture.

The journey begins on the island of Patmos where the exiled Apostle John receives a visionary message from Jesus addressed to seven churches.

PART ONE

PREPARING FOR BATTLE

"When did we start believing that God wants to send us to safe places to do easy things? God wants to send us to dangerous places to do difficult things. He will lead you into the shadowlands where light and darkness clash."

—Mark Batterson

Chapter One

CALLED TO THE WILDERNESS

"God creates out of nothing. Therefore, until a man is nothing, God can make nothing out of him."
–Martin Luther

In the spring of 2006, my wife and I resigned our teaching jobs near Chicago, sold our house and furnishings, and crossed the Atlantic with our 1-year-old son to join an international school in Khartoum, Sudan. When we landed at 7 o'clock in the evening on Christmas Eve, it was still 95 degrees, and we found out later that night the country's capital was experiencing a cool spell.

The next day, after opening a few Christmas presents, we drove around to see the landscape. We kept the windows in the car rolled up so as to not let the heat in. The heat in Sudan is often compared to the exhaust from a jet engine. As we drove, there was little to see except brown sand, brown houses, and brown air from the dust. A few black rocks and colorful plastic bags stuck to thorn bushes were the only colors dotting the landscape.

Our family in Sudan

We later walked our neighborhood streets where the smell of garbage and open-air toilets filled the air. Chaotic, unpaved roads became our charted course. The sounds of children playing or getting yelled at in Arabic were not uncommon. Khartoum was an interesting place indeed.

The Spirit led us to a wilderness experience. Full of excitement, we unknowingly entered an environment that became a place of spiritual transformation.

The wilderness has an important setting in the Bible. God appeared to Moses at the burning bush in the wilderness (Exo. 3:1–6). God taught the children of Israel important lessons while traveling in the wilderness. Elijah encountered God and received instruction in the wilderness (1 Kings 19:3–18). John the Baptist ministered in the wilderness (Mark 1:4). And after being baptized

Jesus was led into the wilderness (Matt. 4:1). God was with all of them in the wilderness the entire time. Each of these wilderness encounters taught new truths or reemphasized old ones and gave special revelations of God.

In Sudan, Jesus revealed himself in overwhelming ways. Through adverse conditions in an unfamiliar environment, we spent extravagant time reading the Bible, praying, and worshiping. In the wilderness, our life as followers of Jesus shifted from a mind to heart experience.

Carl Meadearis in his book *Speaking of Jesus: The Art of Not-Evangelism* wrote, "The kingdom of Jesus has somehow become a religion of the mind rather than a spiritual response of the heart. We focus on psychological compliance rather than spiritual dependence upon the teachings of Jesus and the guidance of the Comforter, the Holy Spirit."[1]

Intimacy with Jesus was experienced in profound ways as we engaged in His plan and spent time in His Word. Luke 24:32 became a favorite Scripture passage. After Jesus left two disciples on the Emmaus road, they said to each other, "Did not our hearts burn within us while he talked to us on the road, while he opened to us the Scriptures?" The travelers were right—when given the right opportunity, Jesus captivates the heart in radical ways. By moving from comfortable surroundings we gained a better awareness of Jesus. Our hearts began to burn "within us" and Scripture came alive.

Francis Chan had similar experiences and gained a wild love for God. He says, "Until just a few years ago I was quite happy with how God was working in me and in the church. Then God began changing my heart."[2] What brought about this change in his life? It came through reading God's Word in the midst of the wilderness in third-world country experiences.

The wilderness is important for spiritual health, renewal, and vision.

In Exile

The Apostle John had a unique wilderness type experience. In his old age, he became a prisoner banished to the island of Patmos by the Roman Emperor Domitian.

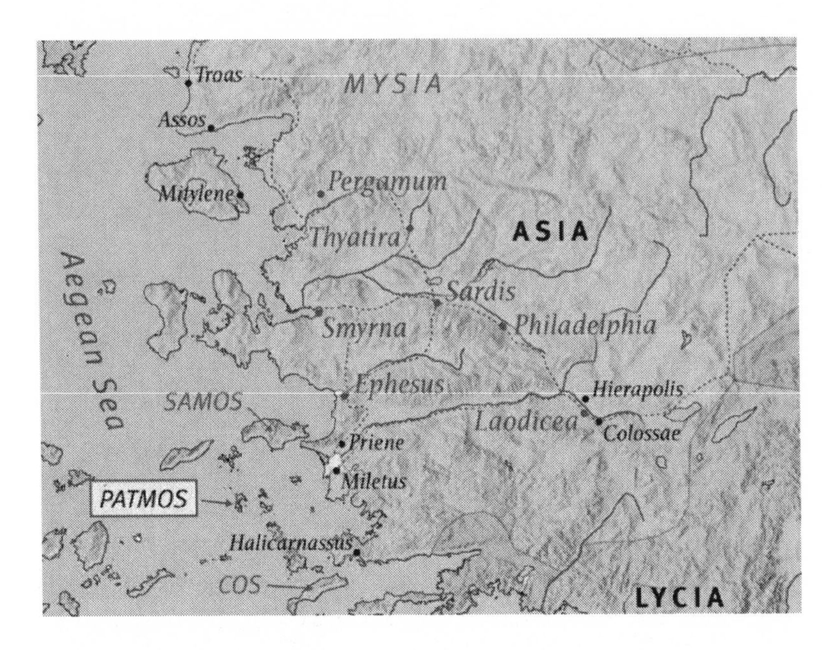

Patmos is a small, rocky place approximately ten miles long and four miles wide in the Aegean Sea off the coast of modern-day Turkey. Romans used the desolate isle for political banishment. The countryside is similar to the Judean wilderness; it is an uninhabited pastureland.

What Domitian meant as a form of punishment became the location for a special encounter with Jesus and a fresh vision of the Church. I wonder if John cried out during sentencing, "Do whatever you want with me, but whatever you do, please, please don't send me to Patmos." Did John seek an opportunity to enjoy God in the wilderness? He once served as pastor of Ephesus. Did he know firsthand what troubles were ahead? Did he know what people would have to face? If so, where would a dedicated believer want to be before such a troublesome situation?

The island of Patmos

Like his Savior, he wanted a lonely place, a secluded place, a wilderness (Mark 6:31–32). Revelation begins with a description of the setting.

> I, John, your brother and partner in the tribulation and the kingdom and the patient endurance that are in Jesus, was on the island called Patmos on account of the word of God and the testimony of Jesus. I was in the Spirit on the Lord's day, and I heard behind me a loud voice like a trumpet saying, "Write what you see in a book and send it to the seven churches, to Ephesus and to Smyrna and to Pergamum and to Thyatira and to Sardis and to Philadelphia and to Laodicea" (Rev. 1:9–11).

Whether by inspiration of the Spirit or by firsthand knowledge, John knew life was going to get much worse in Asia Minor. He needed an encounter with the Lord in the wilderness and a fresh word for the Church for the upcoming days.

The Lord's Day

John declares he had a special encounter on the Lord's Day, the first day of the week. After the resurrection, special honor was given to Sunday. The Lord laid in the tomb on the Sabbath, and the next day rose from the dead triumphant.

The book of Acts records the disciples coming together to break bread "on the first day of the week" (20:7). Sunday was the regular occasion for the early church to love one another in community and celebrate the resurrected life.

In the Spirit

John writes, "I was on the island called Patmos…I was in the Spirit" (Rev. 1:9-10). Located on a lonely, desolate, barren, uninhabited island, John is unable to experience a community of believers. He is isolated in a place seldom visited by others. By this time he is an old man, close to 100 years, wandering a rocky, inhospitable place, yet he is "in the Spirit." His pleasure was fellowship with God. His eyes were fixed on Jesus.

While in a posture of worship, Jesus shows up. John is in a wilderness moment preparing himself to hear from God. He longs for a fresh word for the Church, a special revelation. He does not wait to see Jesus before worshiping; He worships and then sees Him.

On an island prison, John was in the Spirit. In a wilderness experience come divine encounters. In difficult places the Comforter transcends the moment. A glimpse of heaven becomes possible.

Focusing on Jesus

The ability to persevere in times of hardship is directly related to how one sees Jesus. A person must discover how to live in two places at once. Living in a world of conflict and advancing the Kingdom, while praying without ceasing (1 Thess. 5:17) and walking in the Spirit (Gal. 5:16).

Working at the international schools in Sudan and East Jerusalem, my wife and I have had opportunity to work with wonderful volunteer teachers. Leading such selfless individuals has revealed that those keeping focus on Jesus do well in difficult assignments. Those who read the Bible, pray, regularly take time to worship, and commit to a local church have supernatural strength to persevere. The volunteers who try doing the assignment on their own, attempting to lose themselves in their work and refusing to face issues surfaced by God, normally do not last longer than three to six months. They experience a wilderness without God only to find hardship. They fail to gain a much needed glimpse of heaven.

The Wilderness

The wilderness can be barren or lush. John the baptizer ministered in the wilderness north of the Sea of Galilee at the headwaters of the Jordan River, a foliage-filled area. John also ministered in desert-like surroundings along the Jordan Valley. The wilderness is more than brown sands and intense heat. A wilderness is simply an uninhabited, out-of-way place where someone can leave the pressures of life and more intently focus on God.

A spiritual wilderness can take many different shapes. Travel may be included, such as a short-term overseas opportunity, a spiritual retreat alone with God, or an occupational relocation. The experience may involve difficult circumstances like the loss of a loved one, a difficult work environment, tension among close relatives, or family members enduring trials. A wilderness moment comes in many forms, but God will meet us there. He desires to remove what should not remain and transforms us into His image. A renewed vision awaits those willing to traverse the wilderness.

Fresh Vision

John was on Patmos, a lonely, desolate island. He took time on the Lord's Day to worship, and Jesus appeared. Years earlier John was called along with his brother James to walk with Jesus. For three years he heard His teaching and witnessed His miracles. He, along with Peter and James, experienced a transforming moment with the Lord. He sat next to Jesus during the Passover meal and witnessed the crucifixion. He raced with Peter to the empty tomb and was the first to recognize the risen Lord on the shores of Galilee. Now, near the end of his life, seventy years later, John sees the risen Lord once again. Did John break down and cry tears of joy at the sight of his Savior and Lord? John may have fallen asleep in the Garden of Gethsemane but Jesus, who is a faithful, loving friend, showed up in his wilderness. Jesus is present in difficult places and gives fresh vision.

Our View of Jesus

While in a cave on the island of Patmos, on the Lord's Day, John receives a vision for the Church.

> Then I turned to see the voice that was speaking to me, and on turning I saw seven golden lampstands, and in the midst of the lampstands one like a son of man, clothed with a long robe and with a golden sash around his chest. The hairs of his head were white, like white wool, like snow. His eyes were like a flame of fire, his feet were like burnished bronze, refined in a furnace, and his voice was like the roar of many waters. In his right hand he held seven stars, from his mouth came a

sharp two-edged sword, and his face was like the sun shining in full strength. When I saw him, I fell at his feet as though dead. But he laid his right hand on me, saying, 'Fear not, I am the first and the last, and the living one. I died, and behold I am alive forevermore, and I have the keys of Death and Hades.'

After this I looked, and behold, a door standing open in heaven! And the first voice, which I had heard speaking to me like a trumpet, said, 'Come up here, and I will show you what must take place after this.' At once I was in the Spirit, and behold, a throne stood in heaven, with one seated on the throne. And he who sat there had the appearance of jasper and carnelian, and around the throne was a rainbow that had the appearance of an emerald. Around the throne were twenty-four thrones, and seated on the thrones were twenty-four elders, clothed in white garments, with golden crowns on their heads. From the throne came flashes of lightning, and rumblings and peals of thunder, and before the throne were burning seven torches of fire, which are the seven spirits of God, and before the throne there was as it were a sea of glass, like crystal.

And around the throne, on each side of the throne, are four living creatures, full of eyes in front and behind: the first living creature like a lion, the second living creature like an ox, the third living creature with the face of a man, and the fourth living creature like an eagle in flight. And the four living creatures, each of them with six wings, are full of eyes all around and within, and day and night they never cease to say, "Holy, holy, holy, is the Lord God Almighty, who was and is and is to come!"

And whenever the living creatures give glory and honor and thanks to him who is seated on the throne, who lives forever and ever, the twenty-four elders fall down before him who is seated on the throne and worship him who lives forever and ever. They cast their crowns before the throne,

> saying, "Worthy are you, our Lord and God, to receive glory and honor and power, for you created all things, and by your will they existed and were created" (Rev. 1:12–18; 4:1–11).

Life for the churches in Asia Minor was already difficult and about to get worse. They knew following Jesus would be costly. Did they wonder, "Where is He?" The vision gives no details of life becoming easier but lays out various challenges. Christ followers were not going to be popular, and life would not be trouble-free. John saw Jesus in the chaos of his times and in the midst of serious turmoil. Jesus was still identifying with believers but now arrayed with a golden sash across his chest and fire in His eyes. The Father was on the throne surrounded by thunder and lightning. Living creatures were continually crying, "Holy, holy, holy, is the Lord God Almighty." As these letters were read, describing the majesty of Jesus, believers would be reminded of the source of love and devotion. A powerful vision of Jesus and God's throne keeps the Church victorious in the midst of difficult times.

Many knew Jesus as a Galilean sage, an artist creating a beautiful tapestry of the Kingdom of God, a Teacher who went to a cross with thieves and rose from the dead triumphant. An accurate understanding of the powerful risen Lord is necessary in the midst of trying circumstances.

Looking to Jesus

As parents, Shellie and I make every attempt to help our kids keep their eyes on Jesus. When talking with our oldest son about bad dreams, Shellie reminds him Jesus is always with us, helping us handle fear. The Lord also has angel-warriors keeping watch. During one of these nighttime conversations, Nate responded, "I can't wait to see Jesus." Is that our longing as well?

Seeing Jesus

Even if someone has not "seen" Jesus with physical eyes, she can "see" Him with spiritual sight. Peter writes, "Though you have not seen him, you love him. Though you do not now see him, you believe in him and rejoice with joy that is inexpressible and filled with glory" (1 Pet. 1:8).

Not all who profess Christ "see" Jesus. Oswald Chambers explains, "Being saved and seeing Jesus is not the same thing. Many are partakers of God's grace who have never seen Jesus. When once you have seen Jesus, you can never be the same; other things do not appeal as they used to do."[3]

An encounter with Jesus in a wilderness moment changes everything. Life takes on new meaning. The temporal gets pushed aside for the eternal, and the divine vision challenges believers to new heights of glory.

Pursuing Jesus

While serving the international school in East Jerusalem, I had a sense God wanted our family to experience more of Him. Knowing the wilderness is a place of truth and revelation, I hiked a trail at Ein Gedi near the Dead Sea. The place is an oasis in a desert filled with streams, palm trees, and caves. David hid from Saul in this rocky terrain. It is thought Jesus spent forty days in the wilderness about eighteen miles farther north.

Living in a fast-paced makes it a challenge to find quiet moments before God. The psalmist declares, "Be still, and know that I am God" (Psalm 46:10). Encounters with God require intentionally having extended alone times with Him.

Before leaving for Ein Gedi, Shellie and I prayed. While hiking, I sensed more of God because I came prepared for more of Him. The hike was a prayer journey. God was asking my family and me to become full of greater faith and the Holy Spirit. I sang songs expressing hunger for His presence. Scripture promises that if we "draw near to God, and he will draw near to [us]" (James 4:8).

The God not defined by boundaries and locations resides in those calling Him Lord. Believers should passionately pursue the living God. A. W. Tozer writes, "We pursue God because, and only because, He has first put an urge within us that spurs us to the pursuit…The impulse to pursue God originates with God, but the outworking of that impulse is our following hard after Him."[4]

One of the eventual outcomes of my wilderness experience is a multi-site, multi-cultural faith community called New Life Church. About a year after my hike, God put together this church in Jerusalem, followed by a campus in Bethlehem, along with other sites throughout the country prayerfully planned for the future. Without the impulse to faithfully pursue God, would this church now exist? God needs wilderness seekers for His work to become accomplished.

A comment from John the baptizer who ministered just north of Ein Gedi and throughout the Jordan River Valley has become a prayer of mine: "He must increase, but I must decrease" (John 3:30). More of Jesus and less of us! The wilderness is where God does this transformation.

Mission Value: Glorious Deconstruction[5]

Sudan was a difficult place to live, a wilderness experience. We spent four months camping in our house, sleeping on air mattresses, using a single knife, pot, and pan with a borrowed table and chairs from friends. Our shipping container had not arrived yet, and daily we dealt with intense heat, around 115 degrees, as well as trying to learn Arabic so that we could buy food.

I spent a day confined to a police station on account of a car accident. Some time later we remained indoors for days while government troops fought rebels from Darfur. On a trip to visit friends in a different country, we helped them pack and leave because their government toppled. Upon returning to Sudan, the

International Criminal Court indicted Sudan President Omar Al-Bashir for war crimes, causing more problems in the capital.

Traveling home from downtown Khartoum one day, I drove past a Shell station and thought to myself, "If they drop the 'S' from the sign, they would have it right." Living with both heat and hate felt like hell—the worst place possible.

Jesus told His followers that the poor in spirit are blessed with the kingdom of heaven (Matt. 5:3). Poor in spirit refers to spiritual bankruptcy, meaning impoverished by pride, self-assurance, and self-reliance, of consciously knowing misery is attached to the absence of God. The kingdom of heaven is for those seeing themselves dependent on God and pleading for His help. The poor in spirit are empty so God can fill them up.

The Spirit leads people into the wilderness to be made empty and deconstructed. People come into a place of recognizing they need help. Pride, self-assurance, and self-reliance surface, and opportunities are given to address them. A wilderness environment takes people apart and more gloriously puts them back together in Christ. Only what is real survives the wilderness. The unreal dies in the desert. The wilderness is uncomfortable, and individual effort cannot alter it. God is encountered in the wilderness because fewer distractions allow Him to reveal Himself.

After Jesus had a wilderness experience, Luke records, "Jesus returned in the power of the Spirit" (4:14). The wilderness is a place that moves you into a passionate pursuit of Him and His plan, a place providing a fresh vision. Proverbs warns, "Where there is no prophetic vision the people cast off restraint (29:18). In other words, without a godly vision people do not live rightly. Fresh vision from God is important to experience life to the full.

Sudan became the environment for God to reveal our absolute spiritual poverty and greater need of Him. We had to be torn down, reconstructed, and made new in Christ. Growing up in church and being raised in godly homes was not enough to fully grasp our spiritual poverty and complete dependence on God. The wilderness was essential to experience the fullness of life in Jesus, to place complete trust in Him.

The Bible uses several metaphors to refer to the need of being made new, such as entering the refiner's fire (Mal. 3:2–3) and being reworked as clay (Isa. 64:8; Jer. 18:6). Deconstruction is necessary for a person to be fully reliant on God, becoming completely subject to Him and confident in His plan.

Safety and security are top priorities in a Western culture mindset. People often shield their thoughts of uncomfortable consequences. Alicia Britt Chole's book *Anonymous* indicates, "Our earthbound hearts prefer to consider how following God leads us into happiness or health or wealth."[6] Yet this is not the Kingdom way. Paul reminds us, "If then you have been raised with Christ, seek the things that are above, where Christ is, seated at the right hand of God. Set your minds on things that are above, not on things that are on earth" (Col. 3:1–2). People naturally run from the wilderness, not toward it. They shield themselves from the very thing God wants for them, coming to a fuller awareness of His nature and wants.

The Challenge

Embrace wilderness experiences and receive a fresh vision for your life. Wilderness moments are part of spiritual development. In them, a person is challenged to keep his eyes on King Jesus and persevere. "Therefore, since we are surrounded by so great a cloud of witnesses, let us also lay aside every weight, and sin which clings so closely, and let us run with endurance the race that is set before us, looking to Jesus, the founder and perfecter of our faith, who for the joy that was set before him endured the cross, despising the shame, and is seated at the right hand of the throne of God" (Heb. 12:1–2).

It's All About Jesus

The foundation of the Church is Jesus, and the message is all about Him. Jesus in all His glory inspired John to communicate to the Church. The theme of Revelation is the Church on a mission and Jesus is the message (Rev. 1:1). The Church, built on the foundation of the apostles and prophets, has Christ as the cornerstone (Eph. 2:20).

Before Jesus supernaturally appeared to John on the island of Patmos with instructions for seven churches, John traveled with Him during His earthly ministry. During a trip to a remote location far north of His home base, Jesus promised that He would build His Church. It started with the proclamation, "You are the Christ." Since we have come to recognize Him as Lord, we must let Him build us, which sometimes requires wilderness experiences.

Small Group Discussion Starters

1. How has a wilderness experience shaped your life?
2. What are some practical ways to keep your eyes on Jesus and keep your focus on heavenly things?
3. Have you experienced moments of deconstruction? If so, are you willing to share what was accomplished in your life?
4. Sometimes we choose the wilderness, and sometimes the wilderness chooses us. Knowing the benefits of the wilderness, how could you intentionally pursue a wilderness experience?

Consider taking a wilderness experience as a group—take a day for a prayer retreat, sign-up for a short-term opportunity to overseas service, or help someone else through a wilderness moment. Pray for the Lord to give you strength in the wilderness, a greater awareness of His design in your life, and a fresh vision of Him.

Chapter Two

CALLED TO COMMUNITY

"I have community with others and I shall continue to have it only through Jesus Christ. The more genuine and the deeper our community becomes, the more will everything else between us recede, the more clearly and purely will Jesus Christ and his work become the one and only thing that is vital between us. We have one another only through Christ, but through Christ we do have one another, wholly, for eternity."

–Dietrich Bonhoeffer

Living overseas has caused my family to depend more on others. My children have many "aunts" and "uncles" in Africa and Jerusalem. Uncle Dick lives in Egypt and Auntie Heather in

Madagascar. Where we live and the way we live helps us see the benefits of community and understand the importance of working out our faith through community.

Our third child Lucas was born in Jerusalem. At the moment of birth, the Israeli nurses announced, "Mazaltov, bentov le yerushalaim!" ("Congratulations, you have a good son of Jerusalem!"). Yet the weeks leading up to his birth involved some challenges, ending with a Caesarian birth and prolonged recovery. Our faith community embraced the opportunity. They provided meals for two weeks, giving Shellie time to recover and our home time to adjust to a third child. God wants the Church to be family.

The Church

Long before Jesus gave instructions to the Apostle John on the island of Patmos to seven churches, he and Jesus were together in ministry. Jesus brought the disciples to the region of Caesarea Philippi for an important teaching and declared His intentions to build the Church. "And I tell you, you are Peter, and on this rock I will build my church, and the gates of hell shall not prevail against it" (Matt. 16:18).

What does Scripture say about the Church?

- Jesus is the Cornerstone and head of the Church (Psalm 118:22; Col. 1:18).
- Satan works against the Church (Matt. 16:18).
- Followers of Jesus form the Church (Eph. 2:19–22; 1 John 3:1).
- Church members take care of one another (Acts 2:44).
- The Church is similar to a human body (1 Cor. 12:12–13).
- The Church is a family of believers (Gal. 6:10).
- Immoral behavior is unacceptable by her members (Eph. 5:3–4).
- Church leaders are qualified to lead by wholesome character (Titus 1:6–9).

- Joy is connected to God's house (Psalm 122:1).
- The Church sends workers to other lands and cultures (Acts 13:2).
- Every people group is included in the worldwide Church (Col. 3:11).
- The Church is the bride of Christ (Rev. 19:7–8).

The "Called Out Ones"

The word church in Greek is *ekklesia*, meaning "an assembly of people or congregation." It comes from the verb *ekkaleō* meaning "called out." The church is an assembly of people called out with purpose.

Matthew is the only Gospel writer who uses the term ekklesia, and his narrative is referred to as the ecclesiastical Gospel. When Jesus made His declaration to build the Church, He was not referencing a physical structure, but a community of believers.

The early church usually met in informal gatherings and, largely due to persecution, moved from place to place. In AD 313, Constantine instituted freedom of religion throughout the Roman Empire and soon after declared his belief in Christ. Everything changed. Within a decade, buildings called Basilicas where Christians met for religious services were erected. The problem is, as Chuck Miller points out, "Christ did not die for events or buildings."[1]

Where did the name church come from? Germanic cultures used the word *kirika*, or in modern German *kirche*, meaning "house of the lord." Ekklesia was translated as kirche or church.[2] And that stuck.

Andy Stanley tells the story of William Tyndale who replaced the word church with congregation in his Bible translation to better emphasize the community makeup. "Throughout the New Testament, [Tyndale] correctly reflected the Bible's original emphasis on church as a movement rather than a location, on people rather than a building, and on the message of the gospel rather than tradition, liturgy, and hierarchy."[3]

Jesus spoke of "my ekklesia" near Caesarea Philippi. The Church finds her identity in Him. Believers are members of the Messiah's ekklesia, an international group. The Church is a faith community having the divinely expressed purpose of making disciples (Matt. 18:18).

Returning to Relationships

The Church is about relationships and becoming spiritually transformed through community. Chuck Miller writes that,

> Christianity was birthed in Galilee as a relationship. It spread to Greece and became a philosophy. It spread to Rome and became an empire. It spread to Britain and became a culture. It spread to the United States and became an enterprise. We in America must leave behind our church-as-enterprise approach to ministry, return to Galilee, and lead a church that truly is about relationships. It is too tempting and often much easier to measure the effectiveness of ministry by the size of the enterprise rather than by the transformation of individual lives and the richness of the community's fellowship.[4]

The Church Family

God is the Heavenly Father and wants His children to be family. Matthew records Jesus pointing to His disciples and saying, "Here are my mother and my brothers! For whoever does the will of my Father in heaven is my brother and sister and mother" (Matt. 12:49–50).

The church family functions for some people more holistically than their own home. Many come from broken homes, and believers from eastern cultures typically experience a loss of family when choosing to follow Jesus. "The church may be the first truly committed community many people ever participate in."[5] A faith-functioning community is vital to spiritual health.

Some followers of Christ are living under the impression they can simply stand before God with a list of individual accomplishments with little concern for their relationships with others, but can anyone stand before the throne of God only *possessing* claims of achieving much in the name of Jesus? Is it right for a believer to feed the hungry while talking poorly of Christian brothers and sisters? If spending five minutes with believers is a challenge, how do some plan on living with them for eternity? Relationships are eternal, and harmony must be witnessed in the Church today.

David writes in the Psalms, "Behold, how good and pleasant it is when brothers dwell in unity" (Psalm 133:1). Paul encourages the Church: "Always be humble and gentle. Be patient with each other, making allowance for each other's faults because of your love. Make every effort to keep yourselves united in the Spirit, binding yourselves together with peace. For there is one body and one Spirit, just as you have been called to one glorious hope for the future" (Eph. 4:2–4, NLT). John speaks as a brother in Revelation, "I, John, am your brother and your partner in suffering and in God's Kingdom" (1:9).

God designed the faith community. Our brothers and sisters in Christ are a part of our lives by God's divine appointment. They are there to bring out the best in us and for us to bring out the best in them. He means to reveal a greater sense of who we are in Christ by rubbing shoulders with our church family. God dwells in the Church and wants every person to mature in a relational environment. A person may come to Christ alone, but they grow in Christ shoulder-to-shoulder.

As part of a universal community of followers (Col. 3:11), believers need to give priority to closely associating with a local church. People experience genuine family ties as they pray with one another, gain courage from one another, and engage the world with the message of salvation. The local assembly is vital to a wholesome spiritual life.

Understanding God

Six blind men were asked to determine what an elephant looked like by feeling different body parts. One felt the leg and said the elephant is a pillar. One felt the tail and said the elephant is a rope. One felt the trunk and said the elephant is a large snake. One felt the ear and said the elephant is a fan. One felt the belly and said the elephant is a wall. One felt the tusk and said the elephant is a solid pipe. They all gave accurate descriptions. The elephant has all these features.

The global church has taught me much about the character of God. Korean believers teach me about the authority and Lordship of King Jesus. American counterparts remind me of God's blessings and love. Arab Christians give me clarity about God as judge and ruler. Messianic Jewish friends better articulate God's holiness. They all reveal the mosaic of the local church.

A body of believers best reveals God. "All of you together are Christ's body, and each of you is a part of it. Here are some of the parts God has appointed for the Church: first are apostles, second are prophets, third are teachers, then those who do miracles, those who have the gift of healing, those who can help others, those who have the gift of leadership, and those who speak in unknown languages" (1 Cor. 12:27–28).

Various people express God's grace in the Church and believers experience the fullness of His glory through them. Although members of the Church hold different functions, every member is important and instrumental in fulfilling the main task.

A large fishing boat includes a captain, first mate, cook, deckhand, and crewmembers. If the captain asked the first mate to describe his job, the first mate might say, "Pilot the ship." The captain would loudly exclaim, "Wrong!" If the captain asks the cook about their job, the cook may respond, "Make food." The captain would loudly exclaim, "Wrong!" Confused, the first mate and cook wonder, "What is our job?" To catch fish! Similarly, no matter the role within the Church, everyone is a fisher of men (Matt. 4:19). Believers must keep one another focused on the main task.

Genuine Community

Living in genuine community involves holding one another accountable for each other's actions. Jesus refers to the Church in Matthew 18:15–17 (NLT).

> If another believer sins against you, go privately and point out the offense. If the other person listens and confesses it, you have won that person back. But if you are unsuccessful, take one or two others with you and go back again, so that everything you say may be confirmed by two or three witnesses. If the person still refuses to listen, take your case to the church. Then if he or she won't accept the church's decision, treat that person as a pagan or a corrupt tax collector.

Dietrich Bonhoeffer says it well, "Nothing can be more cruel than that leniency which abandons others to their sin. Nothing can be more compassionate than that severe reprimand which calls another Christian in one's community back from the path of sin."[6] A cultural trait shared between my American heritage and Middle-Eastern neighbors is the desire to avoid character confrontation. Yet if a Christian is not living right, avoiding the issue is the most unloving act that a person can do.

Our motivation comes from Matthew 18:14. "So it is not the will of my Father who is in heaven that one of these little ones should perish." This comment precedes Jesus' instructions on keeping each other accountable. Wayward believers are confronted so none should perish. Not living right leads to eternal separation from God. Is there a better reason for establishing genuine community through accountability?

A person becomes vulnerable in compassionate accountability. For accountability to work well, a person must be vulnerable to others and God in relationship. Trusting the faith community and living in a trustworthy manner establishes genuine community. If you trust those keeping you accountable, being vulnerable is easy and genuine relationships are possible.

The writer of Proverbs shares, "As iron sharpens iron, so a friend sharpens a friend" (27:17 NLT). Sharpening character for greater growth and advancement necessitates a willingness to lovingly confront. A genuine friend is persistent and does not shy away from constructive criticism.

Why so much talk on accountability? A church functions poorly without it. Faith communities cannot exist without mutual sharpening. Jesus commended the seven churches recorded in Revelation while challenging them with accountability. The Church is to represent Jesus before the world, and believers need to hold each other accountable for the refining of His qualities and the sharpening of one another's steel.

Loving Your Church Family

Jesus gives these instructions about accountability, "If another believer sins against you, go privately and point out the offense. If the other person listens and confesses it, you have won that person back" (Matt. 18:15 NLT). Sin is initially dealt with sensitively with minimum publicity. Jesus does not instruct members to take the case to leadership. Church members are to take responsibility for the wellbeing of one another. The goal of confrontation is restoration.

If a private conversation is not successful, additional action is prompted. "But if you are unsuccessful, take one or two others with you and go back again, so that everything you say may be confirmed by two or three witnesses" (Matt. 18:16 NLT). Again,

Jesus does not delegate the problem to church leaders. There is no indication of these witnesses holding a leadership position. Everyone is part of the accountability process. The other witnesses confirm the concern is church wide.

The final action involves the entire faith community. "If the person still refuses to listen, take your case to the church. Then if he or she won't accept the church's decision, treat that person as a pagan or a corrupt tax collector" (Matt. 18:17 NLT). Taking the case to the assembly is not about gossip. The church gathers and counsels the wandering believer. He or she is encouraged to repent and then take actions in his or her lifestyle to guard against it happening again. The goal is not pronouncing judgment but appealing for acknowledgement and change.

Anyone unwilling to heed the warning from the church fails to reside in community and loses identity with the church. In Jesus' day pagans and tax collectors were the bottom of the moral scale. Remorseless offenders, outsiders. Jesus instructs the church to suspend normal fellowship.

A family involved in spiritual leadership at our church in Jerusalem, Nick and Angel, were part of a church in Chicago exercising the prescribed process. On Sunday evenings, when attendees were mostly members, the church would occasionally address "final resort" offenses. The offense was presented before the church, and members lovingly encouraged corrective action. If everyone loves His Church, everyone is kept accountable.

False Community Versus Genuine Community

Some may wonder, "What about Joe? That guy is prone to lying. Is he going to keep me accountable? And my friend Diane gossips. Is she going to pull me aside and bring up things I could do better? I don't think so."

Everyone falls short of God's glorious standard (Rom. 3:23). Every church member is responsible to increase His glory in everyone they contact, especially those in Christ. Keeping one another accountable encourages others to be further transformed into the image of God and to more accurately represent Jesus. To move from a false community to a genuine community, accountability and life sharing are required. Those in Christ are to lovingly embrace one another, maximize the ability of one another, and address damaging issues in one another.

Moving From Crowd to Community

Larry Osborne, speaking at James River Church in Springfield, Missouri, suggested the church at large has become something attended rather than something participated in. He stressed that Christianity is a personal relationship, not a private one. Without community, believers have nowhere to live out the "one another's" of Scripture.

It is vital to engage in community for numerous reasons. A person must live in such a way that he is genuinely known, as anonymity and isolation breed sin. One must be lovingly supported when going through difficult circumstances because some situations are too big to go alone. Finally, one must also be honestly challenged and held accountable when one falls short because everyone will fall short. Engaging in community this way provides outside intervention because growth requires outside intervention.[7]

To move from crowd to community, it is necessary for followers of Jesus to make a connection with other believers. This involves being the Church and not simply doing church.

Pursuing Genuine Community

God's plan is community. Sharing life requires selfless attitudes and intentional efforts. When done well, community fulfills and rewards.

> We cannot play at community development—it is essential to who we are and profound enough in its implications to keep us pursuing it until it climaxes in that great communal celebration of Lamb and Bride.... Community is a way of life. We don't like to think of being responsible for others. I like not being my brother's keeper. Nor do I want any other having responsibility for me. Dependency is on the most feared list today. Self-disclosure is relegated to the professionals whom I pay to listen. Vulnerability and weakness are dangerous. Commitment is too binding and controlling. It is easy to settle for a counterfeit or substitute because of the cost to us of pursuing real community. We must not settle for small-group times that are as good as the garden club or the local Alcoholics Anonymous meeting. Community is distinctly Christian.[8]

Living well in a Biblically functioning community is challenging and requires commitment and openness. What is at stake? The ability to reach billions needing Christ! Making a difference in the world requires a unified Church.

The Global Church

One benefit I have found in overseas living is the willingness of various faith groups to work together. Coming alongside my Church of God, Christian and Missionary Alliance (CMA), Baptist, Covenant Church, Nazarene, and other Christian brothers and sisters in Jerusalem is a blessing. When the task is great and the workers are few, we naturally work together for greater kingdom advancement.

Os Guinness points out, "The closer we all are to Jesus, the less significant the labels that once divided us."[9] This was the plan of Jesus for His Church.

Jesus and the Church

In Christ the Church unites. Jesus "makes the whole body fit together perfectly. As each member does a special work, the other parts grow. The whole body ends up healthy and growing, full of love" (Eph. 4:16 NLT). Jesus, while praying in the Garden of Gethsemane, asked His Father to grant unity to the Church.

> I am praying not only for these disciples but also for all who will ever believe in me through their message. I pray that they will all be one, just as you and I are one—as you are in me, Father, and I am in you. And may they be in us so that the world will believe you sent me. I have given them the glory you gave me, so they may be one as we are one. I am in them and you are in me. May they experience such perfect unity that the world will know that you sent me and that you love them as much as you love me (John 17:20–23 NLT).

Revelation records Jesus appearing to John and instructing him to write seven letters to a collective group of churches. The seven letters are not written to individuals. Jesus, the one who builds the Church, appears, walking among seven golden lampstands.

> Then I turned to see the voice that was speaking to me, and on turning I saw seven golden lampstands, and in the midst of the lampstands one like a son of man, clothed with a long robe and with a golden sash around his chest. The hairs of his head were white, like white wool, like snow. His eyes were like a flame of fire, his feet were like burnished bronze, refined in a furnace, and his voice was like the roar of many waters. In his right hand he held seven stars, from his mouth came a sharp two-edged sword, and his face was like the sun shining in full strength (Rev. 1:12–16).

Jesus tells John the lampstands represent seven churches. The church is the light-bearer to a darkened world. Jesus proclaims, "You are the light of the world. A city set on a hill cannot be hidden" (Matt. 5:14). As the lamp lights the surrounding darkness, the Church is to have an illuminating effect upon their environment.

Holding the seven stars in His right hand, Jesus has sovereign control over the Church. From His mouth is a sharp two-edged sword (Rev. 1:16). The authoritative word of Christ overcomes the demands of the world. By handling the Word rightly, the Church will ultimately prevail.

The Word

John begins his Gospel narrative, "In the beginning was the Word, and the Word was with God, and the Word was God" (1:1). Genesis opens with the phrase, "In the beginning" (1:1). By replicating the phrase, John announces a new creation in Jesus. Genesis describes the first creation; John declares a new creation.

Words are how people communicate thoughts and issue commands. Words formulate communication with others. "The Word" reveals that God, by His very nature, communicates with His creation. He is not far off or indifferent. He reveals himself through Jesus, the Word.

The Word is the foundation on which a church stands. A church we attended in Florida put a Bible in the foundation of the church while constructing a new auditorium. When the pastor preaches, he literally is standing on the Word of God.

Paul, giving instruction to Timothy, emphasizes the value of Scripture.

> You have been taught the holy Scriptures from childhood, and they have given you the wisdom to receive the salvation that comes by trusting in Christ Jesus. All Scripture is inspired by God and is useful to teach us what is true and to make us

> realize what is wrong in our lives. It corrects us when we are wrong and teaches us to do what is right. God uses it to prepare and equip his people to do every good work (2 Tim. 3:15–17 NLT).

Properly handling the Bible is necessary in every faith community. Scripture is the measuring rod by which churches evaluate how well they follow and represent Jesus. The Spirit uses the Word of God to mold and shape believers into His image. "And this word continues to work in you who believe" (1 Thess. 2:13).

Scripture is not only meant to be learned, but obeyed. Steve Smith shares, "In some Christian ministry, we assess how mature a believer is based on how much he knows. But the New Testament assesses the maturity of a believer based on how much he obeys."[10]

Jesus declares that if you love Him, you obey His commandments (John 14:15). James states,

> But don't just listen to God's word. You must do what it says. Otherwise, you are only fooling yourselves. For if you listen to the word and don't obey, it is like glancing at your face in a mirror. You see yourself, walk away, and forget what you look like. But if you look carefully into the perfect law that sets you free, and if you do what it says and don't forget what you heard, then God will bless you for doing it (James 1:22–25 NLT).

It is not enough to simply know the Word of God. Believers must also walk in obedience. Some have volumes of Bible knowledge, but the obedience factor is low. Others have little Bible knowledge, but the obedience factor is high. "Obedience is the mark of true discipleship."[11] One of the roles of the church is taking knowledge-based believers and transforming them into obedient-based believers. The testimony of the early church was, "And the word of God continued to increase, and the number of the disciples multiplied greatly in Jerusalem, and a great many of the priests became obedient to the faith" (Acts 6:7). Smith describes the narrative this way, "A significant number of Kingdom multipliers in the Gospels and Acts were 'religious' people who already knew the Scriptures but previously either didn't know Jesus or didn't understand the radical nature of the Kingdom."[12]

It is not enough to know—it is vital to obey. The rebellious human nature and post-modern mindset struggle with obedience. If someone loves Jesus, he obeys His commands. If someone loves the Son of God who willingly came and laid down His life, he walks in obedience to His Word. One command involves loving one's neighbor as oneself (Mark 12:31). Neighbors include the church family.

Mission Value: The Church as Family

I heard at a conference the concept of "I" cultures and "we" cultures. America, as in most western cultures, is an "I" culture. The culture makes decisions without regard to how it affects father, mother, siblings, and neighbors. A person in this culture chooses to represent Jesus without concern about what the family thinks.

Africa and the Middle East are "we" cultures. In most eastern cultures the age-old tradition holds the family in high-esteem. A conscious effort is made to avoid shaming the family. Family needs or the needs of the community decide professions. People of other beliefs often consider following Christ shameful. In this setting, choosing to follow Jesus may involve making a conscious decision to go against the "we" culture.

A young man named Yousef worked as a guard at the school in Sudan. He decided to follow Jesus. When his family found out, his uncles brought him to the local religious authorities. They tried forcing him to deny Christ. The persecution became so severe that the faith community provided a way for him to leave Khartoum. He traveled 500 miles to Darfur and worked with a well-digging crew. There the Christian community took care of him. He found a new family. The Church bears the responsibility to treat followers of Jesus as one of their own. Anything less is uncaring and unscriptural.

The Message

"From the first century through the twenty-first century there has always been a remnant, a group who refused to substitute kirche for the ekklesia of Jesus… There will always be leaders who view the church as a movement with a divinely inspired mission and mandate."[13] Rather than becoming a static building of individually minded believers with surface-level relationships, the Church is to be a community of divinely inspired, globally minded Jesus followers fulfilling His mission throughout the earth.

The Challenge

Be actively involved in a local church, a faith community. Keep one another accountable and be a light to the world.

Small Group Discussion Starters

1. <u>Follow-up from previous discussion:</u> Did anyone walk through a wilderness experience in the last week? If so, were you able to keep your eyes on Jesus?
2. How does your church family compare with your birth family?
3. What are some proactive ways you can live in harmony with your spiritual brothers and sisters?
4. How have people in your church brought out the best in you?
5. What have you learned about God from other believers?
6. What are the actions that Matthew records for lovingly confronting someone in the faith? Why is it important to deal with issues within the church?
7. How do you study and apply God's Word to your life?

As a group, hold each other accountable to community. Pray for God to give greater sensitivity to the Spirit and greater courage to obey!

PART TWO

SHARPENING THE STEEL

"I am wired by nature to love the same toys that the world loves. I start to fit in. I start to love what others love. I start to call earth 'home.' Before you know it, I am calling luxuries 'needs' and using my money just the way unbelievers do. I begin to forget the war. I don't think much about people perishing. Mission and unreached people drop out of my mind. I stop dreaming about the triumphs of grace. I sink into a secular mind-set that looks first to what man can do, not what God can do. It is a terrible sickness. And I thank God for those who have forced me again and again toward a wartime mind-set."

—John Piper

Chapter Three

CALLED TO LOVE

"Go low in foot-washing-like service to one another. Lay down your lives, your privileges, for one another. Love your brothers and sisters across all racial and ethnic lines. Love the weakest and oldest and youngest. Love the disabled. Love the lonely trouble maker. How blessed the church that loves like this!"
–John Piper

Our home is a stone's throw from the wall separating Jerusalem from the West Bank. We regularly see young men climbing over the 20-foot razor wire-laden wall with a ladder on the West Bank side and a rope on the Jerusalem side. Sometimes, patrolling Israel Defense Forces (IDF) soldiers pick them up. The environment is often tense, yet even in this setting we are blessed with friendly neighbors and shopkeepers. They keep an eye out for our family—a great hospitality-driven joy of Middle East culture.

We had a large group of American visitors who came to work with us, which required we rent a couple vans for their transportation needs. The street in front of many of the neighborhood shops was under construction, limiting the amount of parking. I went to pick up shwarma sandwiches for lunch, and the lack of parking spaces added stress to an already stressful day. There were no available spaces in front of the restaurant, so I parked near a grocery store we often visit. A man standing in front of the grocery store gruffly told me I could not park there. I informed him my errand would only take a few minutes, but he continued to argue. So I went inside the store to talk with Mustafa, the owner. The worker continued arguing in Arabic, not knowing I understood what he said. He inferred I was an idiot for parking in front of the store. I became frustrated and said, "Forget you," with a matching waving hand gesture, a sign that signaled he was unimportant and not worth my time. When I exited the store, I noticed a space opened near the restaurant so I moved the van.

As I paid for the shwarmas, the Holy Spirit began to convict me about my actions and treatment of the grocery store clerk. I had to be obedient to what the Holy Spirit was telling me; I needed to apologize and ask for forgiveness. I walked to the grocery store and before I could apologize, the owner offered his apology. He explained that the employee did not know I was from the neighborhood. I expressed my regret to the worker and extended my apology to him for my handling of the situation.

Many years ago Shellie and I were wisely instructed to continually pray for the people God wanted us to serve. The reason? It is really hard to pray for someone without God changing my heart towards that person. Praying for those we live and work with helps sustain the love that brought us to Jerusalem and allows the Holy Spirit to work in our hearts to daily grow and restore that love. If we lose the love for people with whom we work, it is almost impossible to represent the One who first loved them, created and formed them, and died for them.

A Loving Church

During the last meal Jesus shared with His disciples, He declared, "A new commandment I give to you, that you love one another: just as I have loved you, you also are to love one another. By this all people will know that you are my disciples, if you have love for one another" (John 13:34 – 35).

Love for others is an important quality for followers of Jesus. The Church is to be known for love.

Many churches do well loving one another, while others fall short in fulfilling this divine imperative. Even the early church struggled to keep this at the forefront of its mission. In the letters to churches in Asia Minor, the first church addressed, the church in Ephesus, is accused of losing their first love.

Revelation Is Relevant

The last book of the Bible, Revelation, speaks a relevant message vital to the contemporary church. Too often the book's imagery causes many to shy away from reading its content. John Stott shares, "To start reading the Revelation is to step into a strange, unfamiliar world of angels and demons, of lambs, lions, horses, and dragons. Seals are broken, trumpets blown, and the contents of seven bowls poured out on the earth… The whole book appears at first sight to contain a chaotic profusion of weird and mysterious visions."[1]

The subject matter cannot be left alone. The book is a divine revelation, given by God (Rev. 1:1). The book begins by stating it is the revelation of Jesus Christ, a revelation of who Jesus is and His ongoing mission in the world. Knowing the contents of this book presents an opportunity to learn more about Jesus.

In Revelation, John follows instructions to write seven churches with each letter reinforcing an image of ultimate safety, eternal hope, and faithful discipleship. The book targets churches in modern-day Turkey to unveil divine truths. It is an early evaluation of the formation of the Church. These Asian churches represent the local church in every century and continent at all times and in all places. The letters addressed to them reveal what Jesus desires of every faith community.

Just as Jesus speaks a unique word to every individual, the seven churches received different guiding comments. He knows exactly what is happening in each church—their successes, failures, victories, problems, challenges, and difficulties. He knows exactly what is needed and has important instructions for every congregation.

Jesus tells John, "Write what you see in a book and send it to the seven churches, to Ephesus and to Smyrna and to Pergamum and to Thyatira and to Sardis and to Philadelphia and to Laodicea" (Rev. 1:11).

Revelation 2:1–7

"To the angel of the church in Ephesus write: 'The words of him who holds the seven stars in his right hand, who walks among the seven golden lampstands.'

'I know your works, your toil and your patient endurance, and how you cannot bear with those who are evil, but have tested those who call themselves apostles and are not, and found them to be false. I know you are enduring patiently and bearing up for my name's sake, and you have not grown weary. But I have this against you, that you have abandoned the love you had at first. Remember therefore from where you have fallen; repent, and do the works you did at first. If not, I will come to you and remove your lampstand from its place, unless you repent. Yet this you have: you hate the works of the Nicolaitans, which I also hate. He who has an ear, let him hear what the Spirit says to the churches. To the one who conquers I will grant to eat of the tree of life, which is in the paradise of God.'"

Ancient Ephesus

Located on the western shores of Asia Minor (see map), at the convergence of three highways from the north, east, and south, Ephesus was a regional trade center. It was one of the greatest seaports of the ancient world. Located at the mouth of the Cayster River, silting problems plagued the harbor, which required periodic and major dredging operations to keep it open.

Its strategic location made Ephesus an important center for commerce. As a free city, it maintained great political importance, administered justice, and hosted the yearly Pan-Ionian Games. The city was the first in Asia to introduce gladiatorial conflict in a stadium where many Christians were also martyred.

The city of Ephesus was the worship center for the fertility goddess Artemis (Greek) or Diana (Roman). "Thousands made pilgrimages to Ephesus each spring for the annual Artemisia festival, just as Jews traveled to Jerusalem for their feasts."[2] The height of glory was the Temple of Diana, one of the seven wonders of the ancient world. It was a majestic structure where people brought and deposited valuable items, where criminals sought asylum, and where grossly immoral acts took place. Worship at the temple was weird, ecstatic, and hysterical. Worshippers worked themselves into emotional frenzies.

The Ephesians were cosmopolitan and transient people, living in a city with a history of cultural-political change. "The people had the reputation all over Asia of being fickle, superstitious, and immoral."[3] Yet Paul recognized the strategic importance of the location. He stayed longer in this city than in any other place, spending at least two-and-a-half years there doing ministry. He spoke in public settings, visited homes, and saw the message of Jesus spread. Some people may think it is hard to be a Christian in a modern, industrial, and competitive world. But the situation in Ephesus reminds us, Christians had to choose right living from the outset.

The Ephesian Church

Aquila, Priscilla, and later Paul greatly helped the Ephesian church. The believers labored to the point of exhaustion and dealt with hostility from a society at odds with their faith. Disbelieving Jews spoke poorly of the Christian community (Acts 19:9). Seven sons of Sceva invoked the name of Jesus and became overpowered by a man possessed by an evil spirit (v. 16). What an embarrassment, running from the house naked and wounded. Later, Demetrius the silversmith provoked a mob against the Jesus-following community for causing many to turn away from worshiping Artemis and purchasing shrines to this false deity (v. 29). The drastic drop in sales of silver images caused the rioters to fill the massive town theater.

Yet amidst the hostility, the faith community grew and multiplied. The Ephesian church sent believers out to plant more churches. The seven churches of Revelation were essentially one church in seven locations, largely due to the missional training received in Ephesus at the lecture hall of Tyrannus (v. 9).

The theater at Ephesus

Loving Truth

Early in the church's formation, Paul commended the members for loving each other, "Ever since I first heard of your strong faith in the Lord Jesus and your love for God's people everywhere, I have not stopped thanking God for you" (Eph. 1:15, 16 NLT).

Revelation records the church had a low tolerance for false teachers. Acts 19 describes new Christians as no longer practicing sorcery (v. 19). They renounced their activities and burnt, not sold, magical scrolls valued at the equivalent of 50,000 day's wages.[4] Yet their quest for truth and holiness left them without love for God and neighbor. They appeared to become overly critical, losing a quality they first possessed—divine love.

The Church is called to love

Working for God

"I know all the things you do. I have seen your hard work" (Rev. 2:2). The Ephesian church was a busy church, actively serving God in a variety of ways. The toil of the church was famous. The New Testament was originally written in Greek, and the Greek word translated "work" is more accurately described as "weary to the point of exhaustion." The church was not a place focused on entertainment, but on service, sweat, and toil for Jesus.

The Ephesian church distrusted false doctrine and desired to engage in works of faith. The church accurately judged between those abiding in truth and those living falsely. They examined how well people lived like Jesus, but did their toil and careful examination cause the fresh glow of love for God and one another to fade?

Becoming Hardened

The church at Ephesus might have been so busy looking for false teachers that it lost the atmosphere of brotherly love. An overly critical spirit can constantly motivate people to find faults and damage a faith community. The church was devoted and it worked tirelessly—but not with love.

We exist as respondents to Jesus' love. We must not revert simply to right beliefs, structured duties, and cold habits. Slipping into being very busy but spiritually depleted is dangerous.

Has serving Jesus become drudgery? Is your effort no longer a labor of love? Carelessly walking with Jesus can cause hardening. Anyone can easily become annoyed serving people (on account of human faults) and lose godly love. That was my problem with the grocery worker in the neighborhood. When I interacted with this neighbor, other inconveniences had already worn me down. Yet, love for others is paramount for the kingdom to advance.

No one likes being cut off in traffic, lied to, or blamed for things others do wrong. However, the Church cannot have an occasional display of love. She must have a constant and enduring love, even in difficult settings and challenging circumstances. Stott explains, "The endurance of suffering can be hard and bitter if it is not softened and sweetened by love. It is one thing to grit our teeth and clench our fists with Stoical indifference, but quite another to smile in the face of adversity with Christian love."[5] An honest display of godly love is a profound witness to the world around you.

Undying Love

John 3:16 declares, "For God so loved the world, that he gave his only Son." The love God has for the world should be evident in His Church. Love is the first mark of a true and living church.[6]

The Apostle John explains the subject of love,

> "Beloved, let us love one another, for love is from God, and whoever loves has been born of God and knows God. Anyone who does not love does not know God, because God is love…if we love one another, God abides in us and his love is perfected in us. By this we know that we abide in him and he in us, because he has given us his Spirit… So we have come to know and to believe the love that God has for us. God is love, and whoever abides in love abides in God, and God abides in him" (1 John 4:7-8, 12-13, 16).

If a person is without love, he or she is without God, for God is love.

Paul asserts in his first letter to the church in Corinth that love is greater than knowledge, "Knowledge puffs up, but love builds up…if anyone loves God, he is known by God" (1 Cor. 8:1-3). Knowledge concerns things, but love concerns people. Paul also indicates love is greater than faith and hope, "So now faith, hope, and love abide, these three; but the greatest of these is love" (13:13). In some ways faith and hope give more attention to the individual while love addresses the wider community. People are saved by faith and hope, but the kingdom of God depends on love. Love is primary because it unites believers with the one true God, who is everlasting and indestructible.

John continues writing, "We love because he first loved us. If anyone says, 'I love God,' and hates his brother, he is a liar; for he who does not love his brother whom he has seen cannot love God whom he has not seen. And this commandment we have from him: whoever loves God must also love his brother" (1 John 4:19-21). We love others because God first loved us. Believers display God's love to the world because they remember that they were first loved. This is Jesus' admonition to the Ephesian church: Remember where you came from and repent for lacking love. Resume loving God and neighbor (Rev. 2:5). Do once again what made the Church a powerful force for God—things done in response to divine love and activities rooted in compassion. How does the Church maintain that kind of love?

Living Close to Jesus

Maintaining a godly love requires remembering what Jesus did. People should look intently into the depths of their souls and remind themselves of their dependency on Jesus. Remaining poor in spirit and admitting a need for help gives them a daily reminder of their dependence on him! When people have an accurate perception of themselves, they more readily forgive the faults of others. They love because He first loved them.

Another necessary ingredient is living closely to Jesus. Abide in Him daily—and more specifically, remain in the presence of Jesus. This includes reading and memorizing Scripture, praying, singing, and quietly listening.

Abiding is challenging and requires discipline. When my alarm goes off at 4:45 a.m., I do not always want to get out of bed. This morning I turned off the alarm and rolled over. The next time I opened my eyes, the clock read 5:22. I was bummed. I still had time to read and pray, but I missed a solid 30 minutes of abiding time. Rolling over will not happen tomorrow.

My time each morning with Jesus is the best part of the day. As much as I love my wife and three kids, my uninterrupted time with Jesus is irreplaceable. I am reminded that Jesus is the center and my home is found in Him. He is my delight. A. W. Tozer writes in *The Pursuit of God*, "Made as we were in the image of God, we scarcely find it strange to take again our God as our All. God was our original habitat and our hearts cannot but feel at home when they enter again that ancient and beautiful abode."[7]

Love for God and neighbor grows cold when we allow the distractions of this world to take up residence in our hearts. When pursuing the pleasures of this world takes priority over finding satisfaction in the Heavenly Father, the heart is no longer filled with love. The world is not love; God is love. Enthrone Him in your heart and you will love.

Loving as God loves requires abiding in Christ. How do we grow in our love of God? Abide. How do we love difficult people? Abide.

The Message

Are you overly critical of others? Have you made yourself busy "doing" things for God? Have you forgotten to abide in Him?

The Church exists as a respondent of Jesus' love and should not revert to simply right beliefs, structured duties, and meaningless habits.

Be intentional about abiding in Jesus. "Yes, I am the vine; you are the branches. Those who remain in me, and I in them, will produce much fruit" (John 15:5 NLT).

Meditate on God's Word, spend time in prayer, and encourage fellow believers. When abiding in Jesus, the fruit of the Spirit will become evident.

The Holy Spirit produces meaningful qualities in our lives: **love**, joy, peace, patience, kindness, goodness, faithfulness, gentleness, and self-control (Gal. 5:22-23).

The Promise

The promise given to the repentant church in Ephesus is that it will continue as a light in its community and inherit eternal life. Displaying love for God and one another comes with a great reward—followers of Jesus restored to perfect love and spending eternity with God.

Mission Value: Loving Population Centers

Ephesus was as a strategic location. Situated on the western coast of Asia Minor at the convergence of three highways, the city was a strategic center of commerce. Having one of the great seaports of the ancient world made it global. The Pan-Ionian Games drew competitors and crowds from throughout the region.

Tim Keller in his book, *Center Church*, writes, "Paul and other Christian [workers] went to great cities because when Christianity was planted there, it spread regionally (cities were the centers of transportation routes); it also spread globally (cities were multiethnic, international centers, and [new believers] took the gospel back to their homeland); and finally it more readily affected the culture (the centers of learning, law, and government were in the cities)."[8] Paul's time in Ephesus eventually led to several parts of Asia hearing the message of Jesus, both Jews and Greeks (Acts 19:10). The message penetrated cities and villages.[9]

Paul intentionally visited cities and regions of great significance. To summarize his mission strategy:

> In Acts 17, Paul travels to Athens, the *intellectual* center of the Greco-Roman world. In Acts 18, he goes to Corinth, one of the *commercial* centers of the empire. In Acts 19, he arrives in Ephesus, perhaps the Roman world's *religious* center, the hub of many pagan cults and particularly of the imperial cult, with three temples for emperor worship. By the end of Acts, Paul has made it to Rome itself, the empire's capital of *military and political power.*[10]

Reaching cities was vital to the growth of the early church, and Keller makes the claim that "today, cities are more important than ever before."[11]

A global shift is occurring toward cities—not just in North America and Europe, but Africa, Asia, and Latin America.[12] Cities are significant, not only because of their growing size, but with the rise of globalization, they have growing influence. Technology and mobility has "expanded the reach and influence of urban culture."[13] Many universities are in cities where students study and are influenced by the urban setting. They then return home and bring this influence with them. "Cities are like a giant heart—drawing people in and then sending them out."[14] Cities influence the world in a variety of ways.

Maybe you're wondering, "Isn't this a book about getting back to Jesus, and didn't He minister out of the backwoods of Galilee?" Not exactly. Jesus was born in Bethlehem and grew up in Nazareth, but during his three years of ministry, he lived in Capernaum. Today the ancient site of Capernaum has a sign at the entrance saying, "The hometown of Jesus," based on Matthew 4:13: "And leaving Nazareth he [Jesus] went and lived in Capernaum by the sea."

Jesus' ministry mainly took place in the Galilean region. Itself a major transit route for the ancient world, this location was no coincidence. The Levant, which includes Israel, is the land in-between that links Africa, the Arabian Gulf, Asia, and Europe.

Capernaum was especially important. Archeology reveals a Roman garrison was located there, protecting the major imperial highway and the tax collection station. A centurion stationed in Capernaum had a servant healed by Jesus (Luke 7:1-10). As an important interstate, a disciple named Matthew previously collected taxes in the town (Matt. 9:9). Jesus came on the scene at a time when Capernaum was a crossroads, mostly thanks to Rome. Both Jesus and Paul model the importance of ministry at major population centers, well connected by transit ways.

God loves the city if for no other reason than for the sheer number of people living there. Cities are dense population centers where God desires to bring peace and righteousness. Keller asks the compelling question, "How can we not be drawn to such masses of humanity if we care about the same things that God cares about?"[15] *The church called to love is called to population centers.*

The Bible highlights how cities have a capacity toward positive social change. It also demonstrates how they are equally capable of great rebellion against God.[16] Compare Jerusalem and Babel. Babel was a tower established to make a name for itself and the inhabitants (Gen. 11:4). Jerusalem as a city became the place where God's name dwells (1 Kings 14:21). Keller shares,

> Jerusalem is appointed to be an urban culture that is a witness to the nations and a symbol of the future city of God (2 Sam 7:8-16). God directs that the temple be built on Zion, an elevated location within the city, so it rises above the city as its "skyscraper." God's city is different from human cities (like Babel) where skyscrapers are designed for their builders' own prosperity and prominence. By contrast, God's city is "the joy of the whole earth" (Ps 48:2). The city's cultural riches are produced, not for the glory of the producers, but for the joy

> of the entire earth and the honor of God. The urban society in God's plan is based on service, not on selfishness.[17]

The redemption of cities is important to God. Keller says, "From the time of David onward, the prophets speak of God's future world as an urban society."[18] He goes on to explain,

> The great spiritual conflict of history is not between city dwellers and country dwellers but is truly "a tale of two cities." It is a struggle between Babylon, representing the city of man, and Jerusalem, representing the city of God. The earthly city is a metaphor for human life structured without God, created for self-salvation, self-service, and self-glorification. It portrays a scene of exploitation and injustice. But God's city is a society based on his glory and on sacrificial service to God and neighbor. This city offers a scene of peace and righteousness.[19]

God calls Jonah to redeem Nineveh (Jonah 1:2) and for the Jewish exiles to redeem Babylon while living there (Jer. 29:5-7). "Jesus tells his followers that they are a 'city on a hill' (Matt 5:14). Communities of Christ-followers are God's 'city' within every earthly city. They are the renewed people of God (see Isa 32:14; Dan. 9:16)."[20] And God's future arrives in the form of a city. In Revelation 21 and 22, when God's creation and redemptive intentions are fully realized, the result is indeed a city with walls, gates, and streets. All of God's people serve Him in His holy city.[21]

Keller summarizes, "We can be confident that the cities of the world will continue to grow in significance and power. Because of this, they remain just as strategic—if not more so—than they were in the days of Paul and the early church when Christian mission was predominantly urban. I would argue that there is nothing more critical for the evangelical church today than to emphasize and support urban ministry."[22]

The Church needs to reach cities from Jerusalem to London to New York to Hong Kong. Christian communities serving as cities on a hill, redeeming these important cultural, political, social, and religious dense population centers. And in doing so, the Church will impact the world ushering in the day when those calling Jesus Lord will enter God's great global garden city, the New Jerusalem.

The Challenge

Abide in Jesus. Ask Him to ripen the fruit of the Spirit in your life. Display God's love to the world so that others will turn to Him.

Small Group Discussion Starters

1. Follow-up from previous discussion: Did you try to live in better community this past week with fellow church members? If so, what did that look like? Were you successful in applying God's Word to your life?
2. Do you have an example you would be willing to share of a time or incident when love was not evident in your life?
3. If you serve in the church, is it a labor of love or a burden to bear? If it is a labor of love, how has it remained this way? If it is a burden to bear, how can that be changed?
4. The fruit of the Spirit is love, joy, peace, patience, kindness, goodness, faithfulness, gentleness, and self-control. What characteristics do you display well?
5. Scripture tells us that we will know Christians by their fruit, by how they measure up to Jesus. How do you think you measure up to Jesus? What fruit do you need to ask God to ripen in your life?
6. How do you abide in Jesus? What kind of plan can you put in place to make sure you abide in Jesus so that He will abide in you?

As a group hold each other accountable to abiding in Jesus and loving well. Pray and ask God to fill you with a passion to abide in Him daily and to ripen the fruit of the Spirit in your life.

Chapter Four

CALLED TO SUFFER

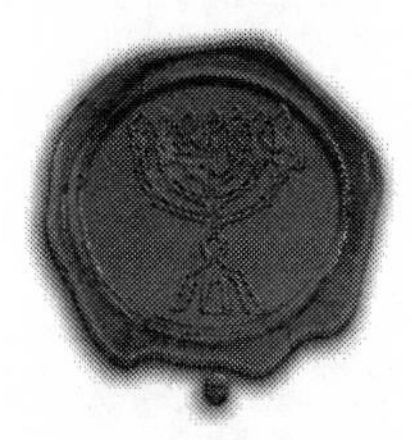

"To be a Christian is not to live a life free of suffering, but rather, suffering should lead us to identify with Jesus, who suffered more than anyone on our behalf."

–Mark Driscoll

New believers living throughout the Middle East, North Africa, and Communist countries were interviewed and asked what they learned from Christians from the West about handling hardships. Their response? Fear![1] When the going got tough, Westerners often evacuated, leaving new believers behind. It is common for believers in the Western Hemisphere to strongly value safety and security. What should the Church value? What does the Bible call believers to?

As Christ followers and church members, we have been called to the wilderness, to community, and to love. The letter to the church in Smyrna shows this can involve suffering.

Revelation 2:8-11

"And to the angel of the church in Smyrna write: The words of the first and the last, who died and came to life. 'I know your tribulation and your poverty (but you are rich) and the slander of those who say that they are Jews and are not, but are a synagogue of Satan. Do not fear what you are about to suffer. Behold, the devil is about to throw some of you into prison, that you may be tested, and for ten days you will have tribulation. Be faithful unto death, and I will give you the crown of life. He who has an ear, let him hear what the Spirit says to the churches. The one who conquers will not be hurt by the second death.'"

Ancient Smyrna

The community of Smyrna is approximately forty miles north of Ephesus on the east shore of the Aegean Sea. It is a harbor town with a roadway extending eastward providing trade with the rich valley nearby. After Paul left Ephesus following the riot, he possibly followed the coastal road north through Smyrna (Acts 20:1). The city was in a great location, and today Izmir, the third most populous city in Turkey, remains an important harbor-town.

Ruins of Smyrna

Smyrna was proud and beautiful with a world-class stadium, library, and public theater. It was likely the home of the poet Homer.[2] The city had temples to various gods and was one of the first places in Asia to establish a cult to Rome, building a shrine for the goddess Roma.[3] William Barclay explains, "The Christians in Smyrna lived in a situation in which on every side the splendors of heathen worship met their eyes."[4]

The city maintained a strong allegiance to Rome and was one of the great centers of Caesar worship. With the threat of death for non-compliance, worshipping the Emperor was compulsory for every Roman citizen. Citizens were required to burn incense and say, "Caesar is Lord." Upon doing so, they received a certificate to verify they fulfilled this annual requirement. Then each individual was free to worship whatever deity he or she liked.

Pliny, a Roman governor in a region north of Smyrna, wrote a letter to the Roman Emperor detailing how some Christians willingly denied their faith.

> "Those who said they neither were nor ever had been Christians, I thought it right to let them go, since they recited a prayer to the gods at my dictation, made supplication with incense and wine to your statue, which I had ordered to be brought into court for the purpose together with the images of the gods, and moreover cursed Christ—things which (so it is said) those who are really Christians cannot be made to do."[5]

Pledging allegiance to Caesar was more about political loyalty than religious adherence.

> All that the Christians had to do was to burn that pinch of incense, say, 'Caesar is Lord', receive their certificate and go away and worship as they pleased. But that is precisely what the Christians [in Smyrna] would not do. They would give no man the name of Lord; that name they would keep for Jesus Christ and Jesus Christ alone. They would not even formally conform. Uncompromisingly the Christians refused to go through the forms of Caesar worship, and therefore the Christians were outlaws, and liable to persecution at any time.[6]

Excommunication

Whenever a Roman ruler died, they were considered divinity. The emperors made the same claims to deity as Jesus, calling themselves lord, savior, creator, and god.[7]

Domitian, the Roman ruler of the time, claimed divinity while he was still alive. He made imperial worship obligatory, exempting only the Jews. Since the Jews had an ancient religion and were formerly independent allies of Rome, they received the free exercise of their religion. Initially, the Roman authorities made no distinction between Christianity from Judaism, and Christians shared the legal protection of Jews.[8]

When a synagogue expelled Christians, Christians lost exemption from Caesar worship and could be executed for not claiming Caesar as lord. Becoming a Christian in Smyrna meant a person took their own life into their hands. Being a Christian was dangerous. The church was a community of heroes.

Early Martyrdom

Some of the most famous martyrs in church history occurred in Smyrna. The name of the city means "myrrh," the sweet smelling spice used for wrapping dead bodies.[9]

Tradition holds that Polycarp, an early church leader brought to faith by John, was instructed to worship Caesar but refused. "Eighty and six years have I served Christ, and He has never done me wrong. How can I blaspheme my King who saved me?" he said. An angry mob grabbed him and placed him on a stake to burn. "It is well," said Polycarp. "I fear not the fire that burns for a season, and after awhile is quenched. Why do you delay? Come, do your will." As the flames of the fire began to burn, he prayed, "I thank You that You have graciously thought me worthy of this day and of this hour, that I may receive a portion in the number of the martyrs, in the cup of Christ." When the flames were miraculously prevented from consuming his body, his executioner ordered him stabbed with a dagger.[10]

Spiritual Wealth

Jesus recognized that the believers in Smyrna were economically poor but spiritually rich. An antagonistic environment towards followers of Jesus made it difficult for them to make a living. Some even had their homes pillaged.[11] Yet as a result of their suffering, they experienced extra grace. The writings of Hebrews were lived out, "When all you owned was taken from you, you accepted it with joy. You knew there were better things waiting for you that will last forever" (Heb. 10:34 NLT).

The willingness of the church to suffer proved the genuineness of their love. What the church in Ephesus lacked, the church in Smyrna proved willing to endure—the church was willing to suffer for Jesus whom they loved.

Promised Persecution

Jesus did not give the church in Smyrna an unrealistic sense of encouragement or any illusions of immediate relief. In fact, He revealed persecution would get worse, but there was an element of comfort in knowing what was to come.

Followers of Jesus are blessed when persecuted. "God blesses you when people mock you and persecute you and lie about you and say all sorts of evil things against you because you are my followers" (Matt. 5:11 NLT). Believers know they will face hardship. "Here on earth you will have many trials and sorrows." However, Jesus gives a comforting word. "But take heart, because I have overcome the world" (John 16:33 NLT). In whatever suffering we may experience, we win!

My dad, in his book *Action: Reflections from the Gospel of Mark*, claims, "If it happened to Jesus, it can happen to you—if they did it to Jesus, they may do it to you."[12]

The apostle Paul faced many challenges including hunger, imprisonment, sleepless nights, flogging, and shipwrecks. His life affirms that believers will be persecuted. "Yes, and everyone who wants to live a godly life in Christ Jesus will suffer persecution" (2 Tim. 3:12 NLT).

The Church is called to suffer

Amidst persecution Jesus tells His disciples not to fear. "Don't be afraid of those who want to kill your body; they cannot touch your soul. Fear only God, who can destroy both soul and body in hell" (Matt. 10:28 NLT). My family and I live in the Middle East, and these words provoke serious reflection. As I watch reports of people killed, often for their faith, near where I live and in neighboring lands, it forces me to reflect on my spiritual walk. Is my focus heavenward or earthbound? My chosen perspective often guides my response between heavenly boldness and earthly fear.

An Uncompromising Church

Why will Christians face persecution? Because nothing provokes the world's opposition more than the gospel of Jesus Christ. The church in Smyrna suffered because it was an uncompromising church.

What about us? John Stott explains, "The ugly truth is that we tend to avoid suffering by compromise…we shrink from suffering."[13] He continues, "Fear of the world has ensnared us. Our tendency is to dilute the gospel and to lower our standards in order not to give offense. We love the praise of our fellow human beings more than the praise of God."[14]

The Church needs a passionate longing and "perfect love" (1 John 4:18) for the things of God, which then casts all fear aside in their pursuit of Jesus.

Choosing Jesus

Even though challenges will come, few people in the West face persecution for choosing to follow Jesus. This is very different for brothers and sisters in Christ who live in cultures highly resistant to His message. For them to decide to accept Jesus as Lord, they may face persecution including the loss of work, family connections, or even their earthly life. Jesus addresses the issue straight on.

> Do not think that I have come to bring peace to the earth. I have not come to bring peace, but a sword. For I have come to set a man against his father, and a daughter against her mother, and a daughter-in-law against her mother-in-law. And a person's enemies will be those of his own household. Whoever loves father or mother more than me is not worthy of me, and whoever loves son or daughter more than me is not worthy of me. And whoever does not take his cross and follow me is not worthy of me. Whoever finds his life will lose it, and whoever loses his life for my sake will find it (Matt. 10:34-39).

Failing to recognize that suffering and persecution come with the message of Christ is to not fully embrace the truths that Jesus taught, lived, suffered, and died for. His message sets the captive free and gives liberty to the oppressed (Luke 4:18). Paul desired to preach Christ and Him crucified (1 Cor. 2:2), giving weight to a presentation of Jesus involving suffering. May the Church give a holistic presentation of the meaning to follow Jesus! Anything less is an insult to the life He modeled.

The Persecuted Church

In the article, "Respected to Irrelevant to Dangerous," the Denison Forum shared, "According to the evangelical group Open Doors, 100 million Christians worldwide today face interrogation, arrest, torture, and/or death because of their religious convictions. Todd Johnson of Gordon-Conwell Theological Seminary documents that 100,000 Christians, 11 per hour, have been killed on average every year of the past decade." [15] The report goes on to explain, "There have been 70 million martyrs since the time of Christ; 45 million of them in the 20th century. In other words, more Christians died for their faith in the last century than in the previous 19 combined."[16]

Voice of the Martyrs lists an online newsroom detailing the stories of persecuted Christians around the world. Pakistan, Tanzania, Iran, Indonesia, Sudan, and Nigeria are just a few of the many places where Christians are persecuted for their faith. In many stories, we read joy in the midst of persecution. James, the brother of Jesus, wrote, "Dear brothers and sisters, when troubles come your way, consider it an opportunity for great joy. For you know that when your faith is tested, your endurance has a chance to grow. So let it grow, for when your endurance is fully developed, you will be perfect and complete, needing nothing" (James 1:2-4 NLT). Walking through difficult circumstances is only joyful if viewed with proper perspective.

A house church leader in China commented in an interview, "Do you know what prison is for us? It is how we get our theological education. Prison in China is for us like seminary is for training church leaders in your country."[17]

Stott writes, "As gold is purified of dross in the furnace, so the fires of persecution can purge our Christian faith and strengthen our Christian character. We need to look beyond the trial to the purpose, beyond the pain of the chastening to its profit."[18]

Why Suffer?

What I have learned in suffering is that the sweetness of the Spirit is poured out in pressure. God on several occasions put me in situations beyond what I had the capacity to handle. Walter Ciszek, a survivor of a Soviet labor camp, explains how I felt:

> I knew that I must abandon myself entirely to the will of the Father and live from now on in this spirit of self-abandonment to God. And I did it... God's will was not hidden somewhere "out there" in the situations in which I found myself; the situations themselves were His will for me. What He wanted was for me to accept these situations from His hands, to let go of the reins and place myself entirely at His disposal.[19]

I learned through hard-to-handle situations that God removed my hard shell of self-protection, providing me an opportunity to trust Him more and making me more in His image. In *Radical*, Platt shares, "God delights in using ordinary Christians who come to the end of themselves and choose to trust in his extraordinary provision."[20]

Elisabeth Elliot gives a brief summary of reasons for suffering in *A Path Through Suffering*, including learning who God is (Psalm 46:1), how to trust and obey (2 Cor. 1:8-9), and being shaped into His image (Rom. 8:29). God's people obtain salvation (2 Tim. 2:10) and gain courage (Phil 1:14). As a result of this, the world is shown what love means (John 14:31) and given a visible representation of the life of Jesus (2 Cor. 4:10). In spite of everything going on in the world today, God is still in control. A Christian walking through hardships with a Christ-like attitude is a witness to the world that Jesus has a golden sash across His chest and eyes like a flame of fire. We suffer for Christ's sake to share in His suffering and glory.[21]

Suffering in Sudan

While living in Sudan, I had the privilege of working with a great Sudanese Christian, Boshra. He served as the school business administrator. If I had a question or needed advice related to living in Khartoum, he was my cultural sage. A couple of years after my family left Sudan, the government started confiscating everything from those working with the school and other Western organizations. Nothing was off limits—cars, laptops, and the like. As the government worked to expel Western workers, Boshra, a Sudanese national, challenged the authorities, allowing Westerners extra time in the country. Eventually the government forced everyone to leave. A few were briefly imprisoned.

Within months of expulsion, the Sudanese government stripped Boshra of his citizenship, though he was born there and never lived anywhere else. He had two weeks to leave the country, which is extremely difficult when a person is not a citizen elsewhere. Boshra had family in Eritrea and attempted to relocate, but his wife was denied entry. The government applied much pressure to Boshra, his wife, and young daughter, and they detained him for long periods but eventually released him. After months of harsh treatment, they put him in jail for two months. The United Nations intervened and secured him entrance into a country of the European Union. Presently, his family is working to secure citizenship and greater freedom to travel in the Middle East and North Africa.

Boshra suffered because he served Jesus. Knowing him the way I do, I imagine he probably smiled while doing so. When asked if I could use his story, he responded, "I am so grateful to the Lord that he made me suffer for His great name's sake." He encouraged me to use his testimony if it will bring glory to God's mighty name. Boshra is an example of what Jesus promised His followers—to be in constant trouble, completely fearless, and absurdly joyful.[22]

Persevering with Hope

Jesus tells the church in Smyrna that persecution can be endured as long as there is hope. Hope leads to joy now and in eternity. Elliot explains, "God's ultimate purpose in all suffering is joy. Scripture is full of songs of praise that came out of great trials."[23]

Jesus speaks to the church in Smyrna as the One "who died and came to life." "The threat of death at any moment hung poised over every Christian in Smyrna, and it must have been an uplifting thing to remember that always with them there was one who had conquered death, one who had taken on the last enemy and who had shattered his power."[24] Divine assurance of everlasting life with God is the greatest hope in life.

Synagogue of Satan

The official title of the synagogue, the congregation, was the synagogue of the Lord (Num. 20:4). "But in some cases the religion of the Jews had become so perverted that the Synagogue was no longer the house of God, but the home of the devil."[25] The Torah, the first five books of the Old Testament, specifies a person should love God and their neighbor (Deut. 6:5; Lev. 19:18), the reason being that everyone is made in the image of God (Gen. 1:27).

Jesus challenged His mostly Jewish audience during the Sermon on the Mount,

> You have heard the law that says, "Love your neighbor" and hate your enemy. But I say, love your enemies! Pray for those who persecute you! In that way, you will be acting as true children of your Father in heaven. For he gives his sunlight to both the evil and the good, and he sends rain on the just and the unjust alike. If you love only those who love you, what reward is there for that? Even corrupt tax collectors do that much. If you are kind only to your friends, how are you

> different from anyone else? Even pagans do that. But you are to be perfect, even as your Father in heaven is perfect (Matt. 5:43-48).

Thousands came to hear Jesus deliver this teaching. Roman soldiers were most likely in the area, watching over the gathering. When Jesus declared, "Love your enemies," the audience would have been looking face-to-face with some of them. Why would Jesus make this bold declaration? Because enemies are also made in the image of God!

Moments before instructing them to love their enemies, Jesus declared, "Do not think that I have come to abolish the Law or the Prophets; I have not come to abolish them but to fulfill them" (Matt. 5:17). The life and message of Jesus fulfill the Torah, Wisdom books, and Prophet writings in the Old Testament.

Jesus later used a parable to illustrate loving a neighbor. He responded to a question ("Who is my neighbor?") by telling the story of the Good Samaritan. The man who asked the question hoped to limit his neighborly responsibility. If Jesus put some parameters on the definition of neighbor, this command would be easier.

The story of the Good Samaritan involves a man left naked and unconscious on the road. Passersby could not tell if he was "one of us" or "one of them" by his clothing or speech. Not knowing his nationality, a priest and a Levite passed by him, but a Samaritan stopped and helped. Jesus asked, "Which of these three proved to be a neighbor?" The obvious answer was, "the one who showed him mercy" (Luke 10:37). The point was, God created the man left for dead in His image. Every person has worth, and men and women of God take responsibility for everyone.

Jesus in His letter to the church in Smyrna refers to the synagogue as the synagogue of Satan. The Jews threw Christians out of the synagogue, stripping the Christians of exemption from the annual "Caesar is Lord" requirement. Expulsion from the synagogue opened them up to job loss, persecution, and possible death. Authentic Jews would have fulfilled the command of loving God and neighbor and not opened Christians up to these attacks.

Missing the Mark

Unfortunately, the Church has not always been the witness Jesus intended. People can easily read and condemn the acts of others without giving true reflection to their own attitudes and actions. Andy Stanley writes,

> What began as a movement, dedicated to carrying the truth of Jesus Christ to every corner of the world, had become insider-focused, hierarchical, ritualized institution that bore little resemblance to its origins. This shift led to an era of church history that can only be described as horrific. The atrocities carried out in the name of the church would be considered terrorism by modern standards. Cruelty wore a cross around its neck. Hypocrisy draped itself in priestly robes. Torture and murder were justified as rites of purification. The church grew rich and powerful. Kings were beholden. The people lived in fear of excommunication.[26]

People fearful of excommunication sounds similar to Smyrna, however this time, the Church was the one not living up to godly standards. Unfortunately, this has happened throughout history—and even within the last 100 years, specifically during the Holocaust. Living in Jerusalem, I have made several visits to Yad Vashem, the Holocaust Museum. It serves as a memorial both for and against the Church. One section details anti-Semitic responses of Christians throughout history leading up to World War II. Another area describes the lack of response from the Church to thwart the atrocity happening during the war.

Even amidst that dismal record are at least two bright spots at the site. The first is The Avenue of the Righteous, containing trees planted in honor of non-Jews who worked to save Jews during the

Holocaust. Names include Oskar Schindler and Corrie ten Boom, a hero of the Christian faith. The second area describes the acts of people like Pastor Andre' Trocme', the spiritual leader of the Protestant congregation in the village of Le Chambon sur Lignon, France. He urged his church to give shelter to "the people of the Bible." The entire community banded together to rescue Jews, viewing it as their Christian obligation. Pressured to cease his rescue activities, the pastor responded, "These people came here for help and for shelter. I am their shepherd. A shepherd does not forsake his flock…I do not know what a Jew is. I know only human beings." Eventually Trocme' was arrested and held for five weeks for his work providing shelter for the persecuted. As a Christ follower, he suffered for the sake of others. His testimony serves as a shining example, one the Church should continue to model.

Church of Satan

If the Church does not fulfill the command to love God and all those made in His image, it is better labeled the Church of Satan than the Church of God. As a Christian, do you welcome every people group? Do you exhibit enduring and sincere love for everyone? Are you willing to walk through difficulties with others? Are you living like Jesus?

Living Like Jesus

During the first Gulf War when most foreigners evacuated Jerusalem, a colleague of mine remained in the area. The school he started remained open, and he transported medical supplies into the West Bank. He stood alongside his Israeli and Palestinian neighbors in a time of conflict. A few years later, the school needed to move into a new building, but the landlord backed out of the deal just before the school year began. They had to move, and the building they used previously was already rented. A man in the area heard about the problem and told my colleague the school could use his building. This man, a grandfather, told his entire family to find someplace else to live, and that building housed the school for a number of years. When my colleague asked the grandfather why he moved his whole family, something not practiced in this part of the world, the man remembered how my colleague stayed during the Gulf War and helped when everyone else left.

A Persevering Church

The church in Smyrna was one of two to receive praise without condemnation (the other was the church in Philadelphia). Of the seven churches in Revelation, only the present day city located at ancient Smyrna still has a Christian church. Nik Ripken, while studying persecuted believers around the world, concludes, "The stronger the persecution, the more significant the spiritual vitality of the believers."[27] The church still in existence at the site of ancient Smyrna is living proof.

The suffering church in Smyrna is the quintessential example of what Joaquin Miller wrote in his poem about Christopher Columbus.[28] Columbus fared the sea for long stretches, unsure of the final outcome, with only the command to "sail on." As storms rose, he and his crew faced them well, for turning to the side would mean disaster. They sailed and sailed amidst dreadful and dreary dark nights to eventually gain a world simply because they were willing to sail on.

Not only did the suffering church in Smyrna last but studies point to suffering as one of the means of church growth. Platt in the foreword of *The Insanity of God* explains that God "brought salvation to the world through Christ, our suffering Savior, and he now spreads salvation in the world through Christians as suffering saints."[29] Is one reason the Church in the West is in decline because it no longer embraces suffering?

The suffering church in Smyrna learned to be a persevering church, holding onto the hope of everlasting life.

The Promise

As Polycarp faced death, he might have been encouraged by the promise Jesus gave to the church, "Be faithful unto death, and I will give you the crown of life… The one who conquers will not be hurt by the second death" (Rev. 2:10-11). Jesus promises a crown of life to those remaining faithful while enduring suffering. Citizens of Smyrna, famous for its games, would easily recognize the imagery of the crown going to the victor. The Christian is a heaven-bound athlete. Part of following Jesus involves perseverance and running the race well (2 Tim. 4:7-8).

The second death—eternal separation from God—will not harm those who overcome. Barclay shares,

> "Fidelity to Christ may bring death on earth, but it brings life in eternity. Infidelity may save a man's life on earth, but in the end it brings something far worse; it brings the death of the soul. The man who is faithful unto death dies to live; but the man who saves his life at the cost of principles and at the price of his loyalty to Christ lives to die."[30]

Jim Elliot wrote in his diary, "He is no fool who gives what he cannot keep to gain that which he cannot lose." Stott concludes, "If we are true, we shall suffer. But let us be faithful and not fear. Jesus Christ, the first and the last, who died and lives again, knows our trials, controls our destiny, and will invest us at the end of the race with the crown of life."[31]

Mission Value: Embracing Hardship

God calls us to a difficult task—taking the message of Jesus to the ends of the earth. Suffering may be required of those brave enough to accept the challenge. "For it has been granted to you that for the sake of Christ you should not only believe in him but also suffer for his sake" (Phil. 1:29). Faith and suffering are bound together as complementary Christian privileges. Yet the benefit suffering creates is greater Kingdom advancement. God can do more in and through a person's life as he or she endures hardships.

Paul writes about this in Philippians,

> Yes, everything else is worthless when compared with the infinite value of knowing Christ Jesus my Lord. For his sake I have discarded everything else, counting it all as garbage, so that I could gain Christ and become one with him. I no longer count on my own righteousness through obeying the law; rather, I become righteous through faith in Christ. For God's way of making us right with himself depends on faith. I want to know Christ and experience the mighty power that raised him from the dead. I want to suffer with him, sharing in his death, so that one way or another I will experience the resurrection from the dead (Phil. 3:8-11 NLT)!

I reflect on Boshra and his family. By sharing in the suffering of Christ, they most assuredly walk in the power of His resurrection, and the capacity for great Kingdom work has grown exponentially in their lives.

If anyone wants the power of resurrection, if anyone wants His glory manifested in great and tremendous ways, then he or she must be willing to identify with Christ's suffering. One must live the crucified life, the "I die daily" life, the "death to self" life in the name of Jesus. C. S. Lewis wrote, "Hardships often prepare ordinary people for an extraordinary destiny."

Suffering either makes one better and bigger, or it makes one bitter. The hot sun has the capacity to melt wax or harden clay. In Christ, become molded like wax. Maintain a right spirit—or harden like clay. The choice is individual, and largely depends on how much one abides in Jesus.

In Romans, Paul writes, "Together with Christ we are heirs of God's glory. But if we are to share his glory, we must also share his suffering. Yet what we suffer now is nothing compared to the glory he will reveal to us later" (Rom. 8:17 NLT). An inherent understanding is that if we evade suffering, we miss out on the glory. Embrace hardships and share in the glory of God.

The Message

Are you afraid of facing hardships? Have you allowed fearful pressures to affect the way you live as a follower of Jesus? Or are you living fearless and faithful with a willingness to trust and obey? Do you have a "sail on," persevering attitude?

The Church can face the future without fear by taking an eternal view about circumstances. There is a crown, a reward, when we come to the finish line. In the end the Church wins. Persecution may come, but trust the First and the Last who promises eternal life to those suffering. As Ripken writes,

> Before we can grasp the full meaning of the Resurrection, we first have to witness or experience crucifixion. If we spend our lives so afraid of suffering, so averse to sacrifice, that we avoid even the risk of persecution or crucifixion, then we might never discover the true wonder, joy and power of a resurrected faith. Ironically, avoiding suffering could be the very thing that prevents us from partnering deeply with the Risen Jesus.[32]

The Challenge

Endure suffering and hardship as part of Kingdom living. Chuck Swindoll pointed out, "The problem with living sacrifices is that they keep crawling off the altar." Do not climb off the altar that

Jesus has you on. An eternal reward is promised to those remaining faithful until the end.

Small Group Discussion Starters

1. Follow-up from previous discussion: Did you have an opportunity to display love, joy, peace, patience, kindness, goodness, or self-control this week? Did you schedule intentional time to abide in Jesus? If so, how did it affect your week?
2. How can you keep a heavenly perspective on life rather than an earthly fear?
3. Has your character been shaped through difficult circumstances? If so, in what ways?
4. Have you ever suffered for reasons connected to following Jesus? If so, did it grow your faith or leave you with some unresolved bitterness?
5. Are you in the habit of crawling off the altar? If so, what can you do to persevere and ensure Christ completes the good work He is doing in you?

As a group hold each other accountable to keep a heavenly perspective during times of trial. Pray for God to give you strength to endure suffering so that you might experience the power of resurrection in your life.

Chapter Five

CALLED TO TRUTH

"The church must suffer for speaking the truth, for pointing out sin, for uprooting sin. No one wants to have a sore spot touched, and therefore a society with so many sores twitches when someone has the courage to touch it and say: 'You have to treat that. You have to get rid of that. Believe in Christ.'"
–Oscar A. Romero

While adjusting to life in Africa, a colleague confronted Shellie and I about our method of coping with change. It is common for those going through the stress of transition to manage stress by controlling their environment. He wanted to speak truth and to help us find freedom. He thought Shellie was trying to control too many things, and that insight was correct. But his reasoning for why she was trying to control the environment was not correct.

My brother jokingly refers to me as having OCD (obsessive-compulsive disorder) because I desire order in life. He jokes about my neatly lined sock drawers and organized closets. My wife, on the other hand, does not need as much order in life. She flows through life much more freely than I do. The reality in Africa was that Shellie tried to control our environment not for her sake, but for mine. I was the one looking for a measure of normalcy on a continent where customs and manners often made everything feel out of control and unmanageable. Shellie was doing her best to provide that normalcy for me at home.

The transition from life in America where things are generally consistent to one in Africa where situations change daily can be profoundly stressful for those accustomed to dependable surroundings. Eventually, I was able to "let go and let God." Now, I still like my socks in the right place, but I learned the value of trusting God more and controlling my environment less.

I realized through the experience that I am a blessed man. I serve the one true God who loves me and knows my name, no matter where I am. I have a wife who loves me and strives to help me during times of stress and transition. And importantly, I am blessed with colleagues who are willing to speak truth even when the words are not easy to hear.

In "preparing for battle," Jesus calls his followers into the wilderness to experience more of God and into community where there is strength in numbers. In "sharpening the steel," believers are called to love God and neighbor, possibly involving some form of suffering. The letter to the church in Pergamum reveals a call to truth.

Revelation 2:12–17

"And to the angel of the church in Pergamum write: 'The words of him who has the sharp two-edged sword.'

'I know where you dwell, where Satan's throne is. Yet you hold fast my name, and you did not deny my faith even in the days of Antipas my faithful witness, who was killed among you, where Satan dwells. But I have a few things against you: you have some there who hold the teaching of Balaam, who taught Balak to put a stumbling block before the sons of Israel, so that they might eat food sacrificed to idols and practice sexual immorality. So also you have some who hold the teaching of the Nicolaitans. Therefore repent. If not, I will come to you soon and war against them with the sword of my mouth. He who has an ear, let him hear what the Spirit says to the churches. To the one who conquers I will give some of the hidden manna, and I will give him a white stone, with a new name written on the stone that no one knows except the one who receives it.'"

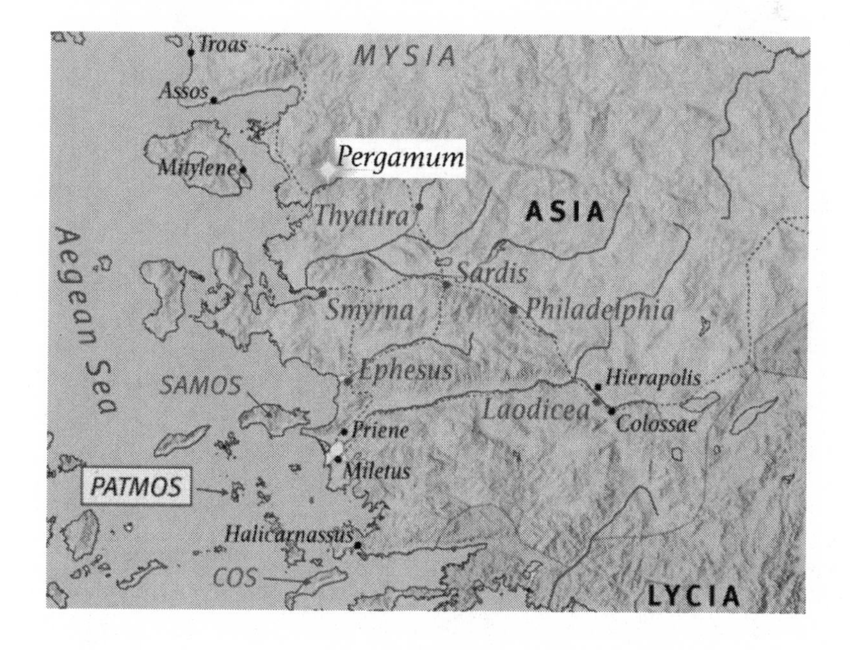

Ancient Pergamum

The inland capital city of Pergamum is about seventy miles north of Smyrna, along the fertile valley of the Caicus River. Built on a hill, a thousand feet high, the city dominated the surrounding area.

As the first capital of the Roman province of Asia, Pergamum had an element of importance. The name means "citadel." The city maintained a 200,000-volume library, second only to the library of Alexandria. (The cities of the early church were all great cultural centers.)

A spectacular part of the city was the upper terrace of the citadel with its sacred and royal buildings, and one remarkable site there was the altar of Zeus, jutting out near the top.

Temple of Trajan at ruins of Pergamum

Pergamum was one of the earliest to establish the Roman imperial cult. Besides imperial worship, the three main religions involved Athena, the goddess of heroic endeavor, Dionysus, the god of royal kings symbolized by a bull, and Asclepius, the savior god of healing represented by a snake.

Asclepius, the god of healing, is normally pictured carrying a serpent around a staff. The temple dedicated to him drew people from distant areas suffering from afflictions. (The snake symbol used in the medical field today may have come from this god of healing.)

View of Acropolis from Sanctuary of Asclepion

Galen, the most famous medical doctor of the second century, was a native of Pergamum.[1] Although the cult of Asclepius ran counter to Christian beliefs of healing in the name of Jesus, Galen had positive things to say about the Christians who drew their faith from the parables of Jesus.[2]

A Sharp, Two-Edged Sword

As the official Asian center for the imperial cult, the city was the first in Asia to receive permission to build a temple dedicated to the worship of a living ruler. For over fifty years emperor worship in the province of Asia was centered in Pergamum until a second temple was built in Smyrna in 26 A.D. The chief priest of the imperial cult lived here.[3] Of the seven cities, Pergamum was where the church was most likely to clash with imperial cultism.

To the church there Jesus is described with "the sharp, two-edged sword." The proconsul of the city was granted the "right of the sword," the power at will to execute. The sovereign Christ reminds the threatened congregation that the ultimate power of life and death belongs to God.

A Bigger View of Jesus

Churches normally ask people if they would like to invite Jesus into their life. "We have taken the infinitely glorious Son of God, who endured the infinitely terrible wrath of God and who now reigns as the infinitely worthy Lord of all, and we have reduced him to a poor, puny Savior who is just begging for us to accept Him. *Accept him?* Do we really think Jesus needs our acceptance? Don't *we* need *him*?"[4]

Is our picture of Jesus too small? We remember Him in Galilee and forget He reigns in heaven. John is on the island of Patmos when Jesus appears in all His glory: "He was wearing a long robe with a gold sash across his chest. His head and his hair were white like wool, as white as snow. And his eyes were like flames of fire. His feet were like polished bronze refined in a furnace, and his voice thundered like mighty ocean waves" (Rev. 1:13–15 NLT).

Jesus tells the church in Pergamum to repent. If not, He will come and war against them with the sword of His mouth (Rev. 2:16).

Francis Frangipane in his book, *The Three Battlegrounds,* talks about the warrior Jesus.

> Of all the names that the heavenly Father could have given His Son, it is most significant that He chose the name 'Jesus,' for Jesus is the Greek form of 'Joshua.' Joshua, you recall, was the Hebrew general who led God's people into war. To be

> prepared for greater victories, we need a greater revelation of Jesus Christ; we need to see Him as He will be revealed in the last moments of this age: a Holy-Warrior, dressed for battle.[5]

How big is our view of Jesus? Is He seen in His current state? He is not simply a poor Galilean but an exalted King. He may have come in a manger but presently sits on a throne.

Isaiah speaking of the exalted Lord, "I saw the Lord sitting upon a throne, high and lifted up; and the train of his robe filled the temple. Above him stood the seraphim [angels]… And one called to another and said: 'Holy, holy, holy is the Lord of hosts; the whole earth is full of his glory!' And the foundation of the thresholds shook at the voice of him who called and the house was filled with smoke" (Isa. 6:1-4). Jesus is in all His glory.

A Loyal Church

King Jesus commends the church for remaining a faithful witness in a pagan community. They had not yielded to the pressure of burning incense to the Roman emperor and declaring, "Caesar is Lord."

The letter to the church in Pergamum begins with the statement, "I know where you dwell, where Satan's throne is" (Rev. 2:13). Pergamum was a dark place. Satan seemingly had a special authority there: Zeus had a throne, a cult used a serpent symbol, and the emperor was worshipped. Was Pergamum the seat of Satan's activity—his throne within the region? William Barclay says it "was a place where the anti-God forces of the universe were at their most authoritative and most powerful."[6]

For believers to live in a location seeing so much activity generated by the chief adversary, is there any wonder martyrdom occurred in Pergamum? Martyr means "to witness." As already explained, to be a witness for Christ sometimes means suffering for Him.

Living in Difficult Places

Although the believers in Pergamum were living in dangerous surroundings, Jesus did not instruct the church to leave. The Greek word John uses for "dwell" infers permanent residence. He did not want them to pack their bags and move to an easier location. Barclay summarizes what Jesus said to Christians in Pergamum,

> "You are living in a city where the influence and the power of Satan are rampant—*and you have got to go on living there.* You cannot escape. You cannot pack your baggage and move off to some place where it is easier to be a Christian…it is no part of the Christian duty to run away from a difficult and a dangerous situation. The Christian aim is not escape from a situation, but conquest of a situation."[7]

Second-century Christian advocates testified that the way in which Christians faced death convinced them of Christianity's truthfulness.[8] Jesus needed the church to serve Him where they were.

We interact in Jerusalem with people of different faiths and beliefs. For local believers, being a Christian in this part of the world is not always easy. Some Arab Christians end up leaving the Holy Land in search of safety and a better life. Another challenge occurs when well-meaning, international Christian organizations take believers from here to "less dangerous, more secure locations." Although commendable, did Jesus ask them to leave? Jesus needs servants where they are, even in difficult places.

Accommodating the World

Although the church at Pergamum remained faithful in the midst of severe opposition, some church members compromised—perhaps to avoid the fate of Antipas. They disregarded the apostolic instructions to "abstain from eating food offered to idols…and from sexual immorality" (Acts 15:29 NLT). Some may even have participated in public festivals and demonstrated support. "Those false teachers who encouraged the Christians of Pergamos to commit fornication were urging them to conform to the accepted standards of the world, and to stop being different."[9]

Did they think facing hardships would serve as a valid excuse? The church claimed to belong to God but was not living right. When any church compares itself with an unchurched counterpart, it begins to justify a less-than-acceptable lifestyle. The issue for the church in Pergamum was not between good and evil, but between truth and error. Jesus is deeply concerned that truth be maintained and spread.[10]

The Church is called to truth

Choosing Jesus often means saying good-bye to past practices. Jesus addressed this with an everyday analogy, "No one puts a piece of unshrunk cloth on an old garment, for the patch tears away from the garment, and a worse tear is made. Neither is new wine put into old wineskins. If it is, the skins burst and the wine is spilled and the skins are destroyed. But new wine is put into fresh wineskins, and so both are preserved" (Matt. 9:16–17). If a person continues in the old way of life, the newly found faith will not survive.

When the apostles and elders gave instruction to new Gentile believers, they simply asked them to "abstain from what has been sacrificed to idols, and from blood, and from what has been strangled, and from sexual immorality. If you keep yourselves from these, you will do well" (Acts 15:29). Pagan cultural practices during the time of the early church included parties, and the early church leaders were saying, "No longer attend pagan public festivals. They are sure to cause you to stumble. They will affect your ability to follow Jesus with all of your heart, soul, and mind." To be in the world and not of the world includes abstaining from environments where faith can be compromised.

I spent my first year of college at a state university not far from Chicago. Shortly after arriving, some older students on my floor invited me to a party. I let them know I did not drink alcohol, but they wanted me to come anyway. Upon arrival, someone handed me a cup of beer. In high school, I participated in the D.A.R.E. (Drug Abuse Resistance Education) role model program for elementary-aged students. As a high school athlete I never used drugs or alcohol. As an 18-year-old college freshman, my stance on alcohol had not changed. While walking through the house, I received several weird looks for not drinking the beer in my hand. After listening to a local band play a few songs, I set down the cup and went back to my dorm. The guys who invited me later admitted they figured I would just participate like everyone else once I was there.

During college, I regularly attended church on Sunday mornings. About a month into the first semester, those same guys came to church with me. Maybe they didn't become regular attendees, but they respected a lifestyle that would not conform to inappropriate surroundings. "In the world and not of the world" means not participating in every activity the world offers. The church in Pergamum was instructed to abstain from the wayward actions of the world.

All Are Guilty

Pergamum had love but did not uphold truth, the opposite of Ephesus. Unless the church returned to truth, Christ would fight against them with the sword of His mouth. Only a portion of the church had compromised, yet everyone was guilty for not taking action against false teaching.

Did some members view the grace of God as a license for immorality (Jude 4)? John Stott writes, "'Just a little idolatry,' they murmured. 'Just a little immorality. We are free. We do not need to go to extremes.'"[11] He continues, "The church in Ephesus hated 'the practices of Nicolaitans' (v. 6), and were commended for their holy hatred... But what was hated in Ephesus was tolerated in Pergamum."[12]

Truth and Love

Scripture blends love and truth. "Love becomes sentimental if it is not strengthened by truth, and truth becomes hard if it is not softened by love"[13]

The Bible gives examples of how to handle truth in love. "Rather, speaking the truth in love, we are to grow up in every way into him who is the head, into Christ" (Eph. 4:15). As a person lovingly speaks truth they become more like Jesus. Too often truth is sidestepped to avoid conflict or controversy, yet truth spoken in love makes an eternal difference.

Truth and Tolerance

Many cultures strongly endorse tolerance. Is it healthy for the Church to embrace this trait? Are truth and tolerance compatible?

Social norms today support people with unbiased tolerance for any lifestyle. The Church should expect conflict when upholding biblical values. When lovingly talking with others about God, the message may not be appreciated, but this does not change a God-given burden to see people rescued from eternal separation with the Creator. Oswald Chambers encourages, "Never be diplomatic and careful with the treasure God gives you."[14]

Tolerance is easy; speaking truth in love is hard. Anyone called to timeless truth is also called to suffer. "As many lonely and embattled Christians know in our own day, it can be strenuous and demanding to live before the Audience of One. Making unpopular stands or speaking uncomfortable words on his behalf can be painful to the point of anguish."[15] As people following the One who brings meaning to life and hope for the future, choose truth and love. Real love leads people to a relationship with God. We have a treasure to give, and tolerance will not save people from hell.

One excuse that churches use for tolerance is the pursuit of relevance. Os Guinness comments, "Nothing is finally relevant except in relation to the true and the eternal… Only truth and eternity give relevance to 'relevance.' To think or do anything simply 'because it's relevant' will always prove to be irrational, dangerous, and a sure road to burnout."[16] Is anything more relevant than the timeless truth of God's Word? The truth of God speaks from outside the situation. We all have blind spots, and the timeless truths of Scripture have great relevance today.

Followers of Jesus must refuse a passive walk through life and refrain from a lifestyle failing to exhibit a meaningful relationship with God. The Church cannot stand by idly and watch people live a life displeasing to God, keeping them separate from Him. The Church cannot afford to tolerate men and women being lost; it must show love and concern for those far from God. The Church needs to value truth and love as Jesus does. Love the truth that "God loved the world so much that he gave his one and only Son, so that everyone who believes in him will not perish but have eternal life" (John 3:16 NLT).

Remember, "The good news appeals far more than it repels, and it repels only to appeal at a far deeper level."[17]

The Promise

God offers His people manna from heaven in place of food offered to idols. God will put bread on the table. In other words, He will take care of you. John Stott explains, "Just as God's people were fed by manna in the wilderness, so today our spiritual hunger is satisfied by Christ, the bread of life."[18]

The church was promised a white stone, a symbol of triumphant faith. The stone is marked with a new name and used as the entrance to the Marriage Supper of the Lamb. A new name marks a new age of eternal communion with the One who has a name above every other name. Barclay summarizes, "Even amidst the perils of Pergamos no one could pluck a Christian from the hand of Christ."[19]

Those who remain faithful and true will be granted a deeper revelation of God.

Mission Value: Disciple of Truth

Jesus, in responding to Pilate, shared, "For this purpose I was born and for this purpose I have come into the world—to bear witness to the truth. Everyone who is of the truth listens to my voice" (John 18:37). Followers of Jesus have an ear to hear the Master's voice of truth.

A person must first hear and respond to the words, "follow me," the request made to the original disciples. The disciples were ordinary people who had jobs, families, and a regular first-century life. Francis Chan comments, "In only a few years, these simple men were standing before some of the most powerful rulers on earth and being accused of 'turn[ing] the world upside down' (Acts 17:6). What began as simple obedience to the call of Jesus ended up changing their lives, and ultimately, the world."[20]

In the New Testament, Jesus gave several instructions about what it meant to be a disciple. He said a person should be a learner or imitator of Him (Luke 6:40; John 8:31), bear fruit (John 15:8), love other disciples (John 13:35), reach the lost (Matt. 28:19-20; John 21:15), and be willing to count the cost (Luke 14:33). Dietrich Bonhoeffer in his classic, *The Cost of Discipleship*, writes, "Christianity without discipleship is always Christianity without Christ."[21]

Even though we are told to be imitators of Jesus, Francis Chan points out, "Somehow many have come to believe that a person can be a 'Christian' without being like Christ... The problem is, many in the church want to 'confess that Jesus is Lord,' yet they don't believe that He is their master."[22]

Following Jesus and becoming His disciple necessitates full devotion to Him and truth. It really comes down to love. "Discipleship means personal, passionate devotion to a Person—our Lord Jesus Christ… To be a disciple is to be a devoted bondservant motivated by love for the Lord Jesus."[23] A disciple loves Jesus and loves truth, because Jesus is truth. He said, "I am the way, and the truth, and the life" (John 14:6).

"Being a disciple of Jesus Christ means that we learn from Him, fellowship with Him, and obey everything He commands us. We study the Bible to learn about who God is, who we are, and what God is doing in our world. The Bible compels us to join God in what He is doing in and around us."[24] It was mentioned previously that Jesus tells the church in Pergamum, "I will come to you soon and war against them with the sword of my mouth" (Rev. 2:16). The sword Jesus refers to is the Word of God, the Bible (Eph. 6:17; Heb. 4:12). Jesus knows that for a church to become a true representation of Him—the truth to the world—it must be led by the Word, and the Word declares we should make disciples.

David Platt explains,

> "From the beginning of Christianity, the natural overflow of being a disciple of Jesus has always been to make disciples of Jesus. 'Follow me,' Jesus said, 'and I will make you fishers of men' (Matt. 4:19)… Yet we have subtly and tragically taken this costly command of Christ to go, baptize, and teach all nations and mutated it into a comfortable call for Christians to come, be baptized, and listen in one location."[25]

Be a disciple-maker! Turn the world upside down by declaring His truth to people in need of a Savior.

The Message

Have you compromised faith? Are you finding it easier to "take on" a life with worldly standards and neglecting biblical truth?

Only truth can defeat error. Between 300 and 400 A.D., a Christian church was built in a temple dedicated to a false god. The church called to truth eventually conquered in Pergamum.

The Challenge

Stand firm in faith and live according to truth. The presence of Jesus should be cherished more than compromised. You can stand up for truth with the assurance of entrance into full fellowship with Jesus for eternity.

Small Group Discussion Starters

1. Follow-up from previous discussion: Did anyone walk through any hardships this past week? If so, did you maintain a heavenward perspective and stay on the altar, allowing God to complete His good work in you?
2. Have you compromised living for Jesus in certain areas of your life? If so, what could you do to reclaim these areas for Him?
3. How are you victoriously living in the world but not of the world?
4. What are some practical ways to become a disciple-maker and lovingly share the truth of the Bible with neighbors, coworkers, and family?

As a group, hold each other accountable to standing firm in the faith. Pray for God to give you wisdom and boldness in becoming a disciple-maker, sharing the truth with others in your life.

Chapter Six

CALLED TO HOLINESS

"The popular notion that the first obligation of the church is to spread the gospel to the uttermost parts of the earth is false. Her first obligation is to be spiritually worthy to spread it."

–A. W. Tozer

Money, sex, and power. If not handled properly, they will cause problems. These three have the ability to both bless and curse a life. Unfortunately, mishandling them causes Christians to live less than acceptable lifestyles. Richard Foster wrote a book addressing the subject in *The Challenge of the Disciplined Life: Christian Reflections on Money, Sex & Power*, and he says, "The crying need today is for people of faith to live faithfully."[1]

While living in Sudan, a colleague encouraged me to install accountability software on my computer as a guardrail against pornography. Even though we lived in a part of the world where women covered from head to toe, I thought it was sound advice. My brother and best friend began receiving weekly reports regarding my Internet use. Knowing anything accessed on my electronic devices was reported to others provided an additional measure of accountability. Even in religiously conservative environments, many people simply live with a sense of false modesty. Issues of sex, power, and money pervade even those cultures.

Following Jesus involves walking through wilderness experiences and living in community. We are to love well, embrace suffering, and apply the sword of truth to our lives. The letter to the church in Thyatira reveals a call to holiness.

Revelation 2:18-29

"And to the angel of the church in Thyatira write: 'The words of the Son of God, who has eyes like a flame of fire, and whose feet are like burnished bronze.'

'I know your works, your love and faith and service and patient endurance, and that your latter works exceed the first. But I have this against you, that you tolerate that woman Jezebel, who calls herself a prophetess and is teaching and seducing my servants to practice sexual immorality and to eat food sacrificed to idols. I gave her time to repent, but she refuses to repent of her sexual immorality. Behold, I will throw her onto a sickbed, and those who commit adultery with her I will throw into great tribulation, unless they repent of her works, and I will strike her children dead. And all the churches will know that I am he who searches mind and heart, and I will give to each of you according to your works. But to the rest of you in Thyatira, who do not hold this teaching, who have not learned what some call the deep things of Satan, to you I say, I do not lay on you any other burden. Only hold fast what you have until I come. The one who conquers and who keeps my works until the end, to him I will give authority over the nations, and he will rule them with a rod of iron, as when earthen pots are broken in pieces, even as I myself have received authority from my Father. And I will give him the morning star. He who has an ear, let him hear what the Spirit says to the churches.'"

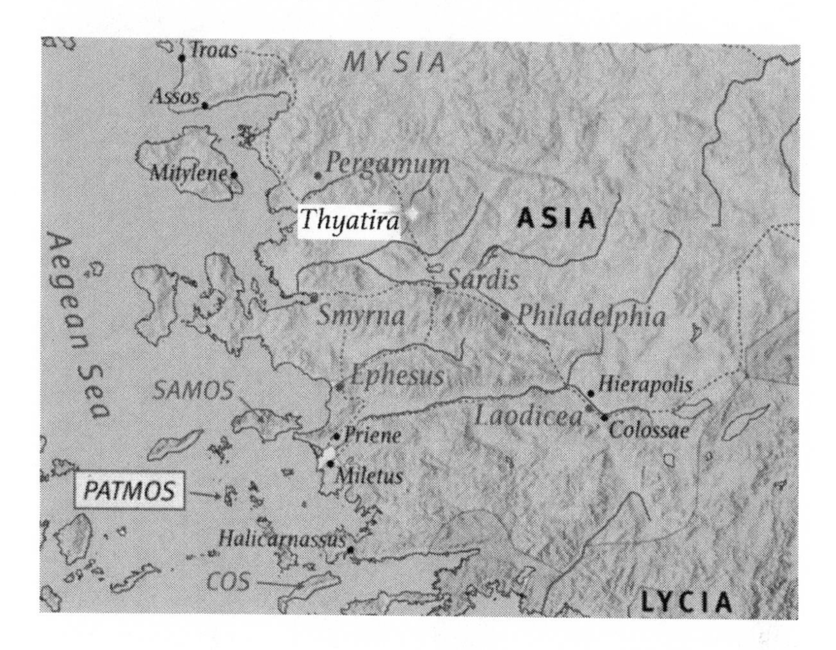

Ancient Thyatira

On the inland route forty-five miles east of Pergamum was the city of Thyatira, situated on the south bank of the Lycus River in the long north-south valley connecting the Caicus and Hermus valleys. The city was midway on the Sardis-Pergamum highway, connecting with a major road running southwest to Smyrna.[2]

The seven churches were each founded in cities along very important trade routes that served as centers of commerce and education. The cities of the early church were impressive cities, but Thyatira was the least of them. The most important feature of Thyatira—it served as the gateway to Pergamum, the capital of Asia.

Ruins of Thyatira

Many inscriptions show Thyatira had more trade guilds than any other town of her size in Asia,[3] important in the commerce of wool, linen, apparel, dyed work, leatherwork, tanning, pottery, bronze-work, and the slave trade. The book of Acts recounts the story of Paul and Silas meeting Lydia near Philippi who was from Thyatira, "a seller of purple goods" (Acts 16:14).

The True Son of God

A growing knowledge of Jesus is important for the life of every believer, and each letter opens with a declaration about Jesus. Thyatira was a local cultic worship center of Apollo Tyrimnos, a son of Zeus. Jesus starts His message to the church as the resurrected Christ, the true Son of God.

Love and Faithfulness

The church understood Christians should grow and develop. Jesus commends the church for their growth in love and faith. For the church in Thyatira, love was manifested in service and faithfulness in perseverance. This was a church of deep devotion and strong character. Faith was proven by living a life triumphantly overcoming the world.[4]

John Stott writes, "Thyatira not only rivaled Ephesus in busy Christian service, but exhibited the love which Ephesus lacked, preserved the faith which was imperiled at Pergamum, and shared with Smyrna the virtue of patient endurance in tribulation."[5]

How does your life compare? You may have started well, but how are you doing now? Have you stalled? Are you moving backward or forward?

Kind Criticism

The structure of most of the seven letters includes affirmation, correction, and a motivating promise. William Barclay shares, "The letter to the Church in Thyatira is to be a letter of warning and of criticism, and yet it begins with a verse of undiluted praise… Real criticism must always encourage and never discourage."[6] Within these letters Jesus gives advice about addressing others. Confront issues, but do so for the good of the person. Discuss matters in ways that show love and concern lies behind any criticism, hoping a person might become more like Jesus and exhibit His character in everything said and done.

Desiring Prosperity

Jesus says, "This I have against you, you tolerate." This letter is a message against tolerance of sin within the church. Jesus condemned participating in social events, eating food sacrificed to idols, and participating in sexual immorality. Trade guilds hosted pagan religious practices as the criteria for membership, and these guilds dominated the economic life of the city. Christians faced social rejection and economic hardship by abstaining from things dedicated to pagan deities.

In Thyatira, if the Christian merchant, trader, or craftsman was a member of a trade-guild and participant in their ceremonies, the person protected their business interests and ensured material prosperity. If they refused membership in a guild and refused participation in the ceremonies, these Christian merchants would be committing commercial suicide and would likely face poverty and possibly bankruptcy.[7] The Church is always tempted to compromise—Christianity costs something and Jesus is worth any sacrifice.

The church in Smyrna suffered imprisonment for choosing Jesus. Yet, suffering often produces holiness, something the church in Thyatira lacked. Elisabeth Elliot explains, "Suffering creates the possibility of growth in holiness, but only to those who, by letting all else go, are open to the training-not by arguing with the Lord about what they did or did not do to deserve punishment, but by praying, 'Lord, show me what You have for me in this.'"[8]

Jesus Our Treasure

Jesus gives an analogy about the joy of following Him:

> "The kingdom of heaven is like treasure hidden in a field, which a man found and covered up. Then in his joy he goes and sells all that he has and buys that field. Again, the kingdom of heaven is like a merchant in search of fine pearls, who, on finding one pearl of great value, went and sold all that he had and bought it" (Matt. 13:44-46).

The person joyfully sold everything to buy the field. Serving Jesus, no matter the cost, is always a joyful surrender if done from the perspective that Jesus is our treasure. The church in Thyatira tolerated because they would not accept the cost of following Jesus.

Following a Jezebel

Jezebel symbolizes the detrimental powers of false religion among the people of God. In Pergamum the compromise came from outside the church, whereas in Thyatira someone within the church initiated and encouraged the same compromise. The person may have argued or insisted that Christians should become members of the trade guilds, that they should attend parties and compromise to protect business interests.[9]

The trade guilds held their banquets in pagan temples. After eating, those in attendance often engaged in sexually immoral acts on the couches where they reclined.[10] The Jezebel individual was unwilling to let go of an alliance with the pagan environment and influenced others to follow similar practices, leaving the church less than holy. Peter's admonition to be holy just as God is holy was neglected (1 Peter 1:16).

They changed the Word of God to suit the environment and their desire for prosperity based on the standards of the town. The church in Thyatira, along with the others, was given instruction to not eat food sacrificed to idols and to remain sexually pure. Living in a town heavily influenced by trade guilds challenged this notion. The Jezebel individual seemed to influence members within the church saying grace would cover these practices. Paul wrote the church in Rome, "What shall we say then? Are we to continue in sin that grace may abound? By no means! How can we who died to sin still live in it" (Rom. 6:1-2)? Believers experience a new life in Jesus where they no longer are slaves to sin. Paul continues, "Let not sin therefore reign in your mortal body, to make you obey its passions" (v. 12). Christians have been set free in order to live holy lives.

The Church is called to holiness

Paul writes, "God has called us to live holy lives, not impure lives" (1 Thess. 4:7). "The Bible…is passionately concerned about what kind of people they are who claim to be the people of God."[11] To be in the presence of God requires holiness. Worshipping God includes holiness. We are to present our "bodies as a living sacrifice, holy and acceptable to God" as part of our spiritual worship (Rom. 12:1). If the enemy cannot destroy the church by persecution or false beliefs, he tries to corrupt it with evil practices.[12]

Deception from Within

The issue for the church in Thyatira came from inside the church, from somebody proposing to deal with the world through compromise. The letter to this church is the longest of the seven letters because deception from within must be seriously challenged. The woodpeckers inside Noah's Ark had to be far more dangerous to the boat than the storm outside. Deceptive people within the church can be much more dangerous than challenges faced outside her walls.

A Compromised Life

During my high school years, the Christian band DC Talk came out with the song "What If I Stumble?" It opens with the declaration: "The greatest single cause of atheism in the world today is Christians who acknowledge Jesus with their lips, then walk out the door and deny him by their lifestyle. That is what an unbelieving world simply finds unbelievable." The chorus goes on to proclaim, "What if I stumble, what if I fall? What if I lose my step, and I make fools of us all?"[13] Christians who choose to compromise do not represent Jesus well.

Church history demonstrates the Church was better at policing the behavior of outsiders than policing her own.[14] Holding one another accountable to godly living should be a priority for those within the Church.

Unfortunately there have been many examples of Christians falling short of godly standards. Peter counsels, "Be sober-minded; be watchful. Your adversary the devil prowls around like a roaring lion, seeking someone to devour" (1 Peter 5:8). The enemy works to defeat the church by any means possible. A compromised lifestyle is one of his tactics.

Is your life holy and acceptable to God? Are you a living witness to the message of Jesus?

Examining the Heart

People often persuade themselves that their wrongdoing is hidden and will never come to light. The Bible says differently. Jeremiah declares, "But I, the Lord, search all hearts and examine secret motives. I give all people their due rewards, according to what their actions deserve" (Jer. 17:10). To the church in Thyatira, Jesus introduces himself as one "who has eyes like a flame of fire" (Rev. 2:18). Jesus examines the heart and "will judge all people according to their deeds" (Matt. 16:27).

"Living in the fear of the Lord" (2 Cor. 7:1) understands God sees all. "He sees our sitting and our rising, and perceives our thoughts from afar. We cannot escape from his presence. His all-seeing eye is always upon us. To remember this is a most powerful stimulus to holy living."[15] Having a clean heart before God is important. Jesus is the only one who can cleanse us in a way to bear the gaze of His eyes.[16]

Unrepentant Heart

Coming before God with repentance is essential. The strongest threat to Jezebel and the other offenders was their reluctance to repent. Christianity is about repentance—about our own repentance and about calling others to repent.

Jesus in the Sermon on the Mount says God blesses those who mourn (Matt. 5:4). A blessing is connected to mourning over sin, possessing heartbreaking sorrow, unhidden sadness, and feeling about sin the same way as God.

Those who do not follow Jesus respond to sin in various ways: denying, justifying, hiding, or bearing apathy toward it. Or they are only sorry if caught. Was this the response of those in the church at Thyatira? Godly repentance and mourning over sin are seen in those who genuinely follow Christ.

King David after being confronted by the prophet Nathan about his adulterous and murderous acts provides an example of repentance. Nathan pronounces judgment on David and he responds, "'I have sinned against the Lord.' And Nathan said to David, 'The Lord also has put away your sin'" (2 Sam. 12:13). David then writes a beautiful Psalm in response to the confrontation by Nathan:

> Have mercy on me, O God, according to your steadfast love; according to your abundant mercy blot out my transgressions. Wash me thoroughly from my iniquity, and cleanse me from my sin!
>
> For I know my transgressions, and my sin is ever before me. Against you, you only, have I sinned and done what is evil in your sight, so that you may be justified in your words and blameless in your judgment. Behold, I was brought forth in iniquity, and in sin did my mother conceive me. Behold, you delight in truth in the inward being, and you teach me wisdom in the secret heart.

> Purge me with hyssop, and I shall be clean; wash me, and I shall be whiter than snow. Let me hear joy and gladness; let the bones that you have broken rejoice. Hide your face from my sins, and blot out all my iniquities. Create in me a clean heart, O God, and renew a right spirit within me. Cast me not away from your presence, and take not your Holy Spirit from me. Restore to me the joy of your salvation, and uphold me with a willing spirit.
>
> Then I will teach transgressors your ways, and sinners will return to you. Deliver me from bloodguiltiness, O God, O God of my salvation, and my tongue will sing aloud of your righteousness. O Lord, open my lips, and my mouth will declare your praise. For you will not delight in sacrifice, or I would give it; you will not be pleased with a burnt offering. The sacrifices of God are a broken spirit; a broken and contrite heart, O God, you will not despise. (Psalm 51:1-17)

David's confession leads to God's forgiveness. He asks God to create a clean heart, not to be cast from the Lord's presence, and to restore the joy of his salvation. He wants the *Holy* Spirit to remain. How can He remain if someone is not living a *holy* life? David goes on to explain the sacrifice God wants is a broken spirit and contrite heart. Are we willing to confess our sin in order to find forgiveness, the longing of the soul? The result is finding the joy only God can bring.

"The Christian life does not consist in one victory over sin; it consists in a life-long fidelity which defies every assault of sin. The Christian life is not a battle; it is a campaign."[17] The Lord is walking among the Church, judging evil, but also offering deliverance to the fallen if they repent. We must stop doing the deeds of Jezebel and hold onto the teachings we received.

The Promise

Jesus promises the same authority that He was granted from the Father to those remaining holy. Overcomers are promised the morning star, victory in Jesus in a darkened world, and a clearer revelation of Him. "As the morning star rises over the darkness of the night, so the Christian will rise over the darkness of death. The Christian life, even at its hardest and its darkest, looks, not to the sunset, but to the dawn."[18] Revelation 22:16 reveals Jesus as the bright morning star. When Jesus pledges to give "the one who conquers" this star, He is pledging to them himself. Rejecting Jezebel leads to receiving Jesus.

The church in Thyatira eventually conquered—they followed Jesus instead of Jezebel. By the year 200, the city was completely Christian.[19]

Mission Value: Active Holiness

Paul writes in Romans, "Present your bodies as a living sacrifice, holy and acceptable to God, which is your spiritual worship. Do not be conformed to this world, but be transformed by the renewal of your mind, that by testing you may discern what is the will of God, what is good and acceptable and perfect" (Rom. 12:1-2). Active holiness is an intentional effort to become more like Jesus.

Becoming more like Christ is difficult because of a sinful nature. Paul addresses this: "I do not understand my own actions. For I do not do what I want, but I do the very thing I hate… For I have the desire to do what is right, but not the ability to carry it out. For I do not do the good I want, but the evil I do not want is what I keep on doing" (Rom. 7:15, 18-19). In other words, there is a war that rages within us. By following Jesus, we want to do right, but our sin nature wants to rule. The question is, will we work with the Spirit to overcome, to conquer our sin nature? In doing so, we become more like Jesus. This is what Paul refers to when he encourages the church in Corinth to "take every thought captive to obey Christ" (2 Cor. 10:5).

Pat Rusch, a pastor in Michigan, developed a series that deals with this issue. (I hope he puts this into book form one day.) He kindly allowed me to summarize his thoughts. We have a need for a renewed mind. We live by a set of established internal principles. They define our interpretation of life, drive our choices, and determine our behavior. Issues that a person faces while following Jesus often are the result of a mind not renewed. Experiencing renewal involves refusing to conform to the world and becoming transformed. Renewing the mind will not come through willpower, self-help, legalism, or any other method. The power and quality of your spiritual life will never exceed the level of your transformation in Christ.

Transformation needs to occur in a person's spirit, soul, and body—your soul being comprised of your mind, will, and emotions. When someone chooses Jesus and lives a surrendered life, their spirit is transformed and the potential for a renewed body and soul is granted through the work of the Holy Spirit. A person cannot *add* Jesus to their life—He must take over. Paul writes, "This means that anyone who belongs to Christ has become a new person. The old life is gone; a new life has begun" (2 Cor. 5:17 NLT)! The person is now born of God's seed. "You have been born again, not of perishable seed but of imperishable, through the living and abiding word of God" (1 Peter 1:23). And this changes the way a person lives. "No one born of God makes a practice of sinning, for God's seed abides in him, and he cannot keep on sinning because he has been born of God" (1 John 3:9).

When Pastor Pat discussed this with a genetics expert at the University of Minnesota, the professor said that being born of God's seed, as described in Scripture, literally means becoming a brand new creation, a child of God, and a part of an entirely new race having all of God's nature. From the moment of conception, all that He is resides in us with its full potential. When we decide to follow Jesus and dedicate our lives to Him, God imparts a divine blueprint. All of the character and attributes of God—His knowledge, holiness, power, faithfulness, goodness, grace, mercy, compassion, hatred of sin, understanding, wisdom, and creativity—become a part of our spiritual DNA. We do not become little gods but have the power to become godly. All of the fruit of the Spirit—

love, joy, peace, patience, kindness, goodness, faithfulness, gentleness, and self-control—are in seed form, willing to germinate and mature.

This is what Paul refers to in Galatians, "I have been crucified with Christ. It is no longer I who live, but Christ who lives in me" (Gal. 2:20). We simply need to say "no" to the sinful nature and allow the character of Jesus to live through us. Sin chooses selfishness, but a divine DNA is love. In our old life we may have suffered fear and anxiety, but in Jesus we can find contentment, confidence, and security. Christianity is an outliving of an indwelling Christ.[20] Paul declares, "For it is God who works in you, both to will and to work for his good pleasure" (Phil. 2:13).

Choosing to follow Jesus may not immediately renew a person's mind, but it gives the potential and power to pursue a renewed mind. The process of renewing one's mind, as laid out by Pastor Pat, involves five steps. A person must first realize he has an issue. He then recognizes that the emotion or thought is inconsistent with the character of Christ. Upon that recognition, a person must choose to renounce or reject the unhealthy emotion or thought. The fourth step is releasing and surrendering the thought or emotion. Let it go! And by doing so, part of the old self dies. The final step is renewal. By releasing the old self and meditating on God's truth, His seed germinates in one's life. Still, a person must choose to live in the Spirit. Paul instructs, "Those who live according to the flesh set their minds on the things of the flesh, but those who live according to the Spirit set their minds on the things of the Spirit" (Rom. 8:5).

Holiness is not defined by what we *cannot do* but simply by what we *do not do* because we are made new in Christ. By God's help we live in community because the Triune God lives in community. In Jesus' name we love because God is love. We suffer because Jesus suffered. We walk in truth because God is truth. We are holy because God is holy. The issue is not that we *can't* look at pornograghy, cheat on finances, and misuse power in leadership. Rather, we *do not do* those things because of who we are in Christ.

In Jesus we have a divine blueprint with the ability to set our minds on the things of the Spirit. With His God-seed germinating and producing His character in us, we choose to realize, recognize, renounce, release, and be renewed in His name.

The Message

Disloyalty occurs by both compromise without and deception within. Rather than changing the Word of God, let the Word of God change you.

Are you failing to be loyal to Christ? Are you caught up in unwholesome practices turning you away from God?

Remain steadfast in faith and continue walking in accordance to His will. Be committed to a process of renewal allowing godly character to rule your life.

The Challenge

Remain holy as God is holy. As you engage the world, stay loyal to Jesus. He is worth it.

Small Group Discussion Starters

1. Follow-up from previous discussion: In what ways could you have lived more like Jesus this week? How were you able to live in the world but not be a part of it? Who are you helping become more like Jesus?
2. How does Jesus model the proper way to correct someone?
3. Is the Holy Spirit speaking to you about some things you tolerate in your life?
4. How do you mourn over sin in your life? When do you approach God with a repentant heart and a desire for genuine change?

5. How do you engage the Word of God and allow it to change you from the inside out?
6. What emotions, thoughts, or wills do you need to surrender to Jesus to be renewed?

As a group, hold each other accountable to live holy lives. Ask the Holy Spirit to reveal matters in your life that need to be dealt with. Then go before God with a Psalm 51 repentant heart seeking the renewal that only He can bring.

Chapter Seven

CALLED TO AUTHENTICITY

"If today's church does not recapture the sacrificial spirit of the early church, it will lose its authenticity, forfeit the loyalty of millions, and be dismissed as an irrelevant social club with no meaning."
–Martin Luther King, Jr.

Our work overseas limits our ability to form concrete relationships. We make friends fast and have deep conversations. We never know when we'll see each other again.

Some people make an impression quickly. Several years ago I met such a person. His name was Stan, and he was a man who loved his wife, family, and work. A few months after getting acquainted, I received a message from him. He had Stage 4 cancer and, even with chemotherapy, was given only a few months to live.

I wept for his family, prayed for healing, and struggled with what this meant for his work.

Paul declares, "For to me to live is Christ, and to die is gain. If I am to live in the flesh, that means fruitful labor for me. Yet which I shall choose I cannot tell. I am hard pressed between the two. My desire is to depart and be with Christ, for that is far better. But to remain in the flesh is more necessary on your account" (Phil. 1:21-24). I knew God would be pleased having Stan in His presence and Stan would be blessed being in the presence of the Lord. He dedicated his life to and lived for Jesus. Yet those left behind would experience a sense of loss. He loved his wife, two kids, and the work God gave him to do.

His email asked for prayer. He wanted wisdom about chemotherapy. If the treatment would give additional months to tell others about Jesus, he wanted strength. If the procedure would hinder an ability to work for God, he preferred to skip it. How should someone respond to such a request?

If you spend time in the presence of Jesus, sing songs of praise, meditate on Scripture, and talk with Him regularly, you either want to serve Him or go be with Him. Stan had no regrets. His life had been well lived. His prayer aligned with a desire to have his remaining days filled with opportunities for Jesus. He maintained an authentic relationship with His Savior.

In a book that chronicles Stan's life, *Dying Out Loud*, he wrote, "It's very easy these days for American Christians to live a good life, to serve their church and their community, and do good things. But sometimes there's a big difference between living a good life and living the life God has prepared for you."[1]

While preparing for battle, we are called to wilderness experiences and genuine community. In a setting where believers challenge one another, described as sharpening steel, we are called to love, find value in suffering, live in truth, and walk in holiness. The letter to the church in Sardis reveals the call to authenticity.

Revelation 3:1-6

"And to the angel of the church in Sardis write: 'The words of him who has the seven spirits of God and the seven stars.'

'I know your works. You have the reputation of being alive, but you are dead. Wake up, and strengthen what remains and is about to die, for I have not found your works complete in the sight of my God. Remember, then, what you received and heard. Keep it, and repent. If you will not wake up, I will come like a thief, and you will not know at what hour I will come against you. Yet you have still a few names in Sardis, people who have not soiled their garments, and they will walk with me in white, for they are worthy. The one who conquers will be clothed thus in white garments, and I will never blot his name out of the book of life. I will confess his name before my Father and before his angels. He who has an ear, let him hear what the Spirit says to the churches.'"

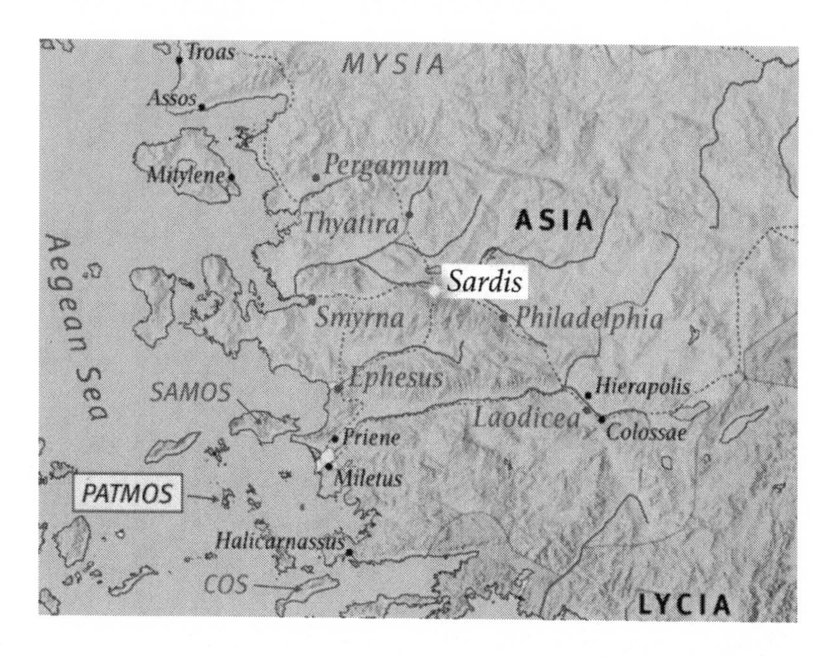

Ancient Sardis

Sardis was thirty miles south of Thyatira and fifty miles east of Smyrna on a northern spur of Mt. Tmolus, overlooking the broad and fertile plain of the Hermus. The city was settled before the Trojan War, as early as 1400 B.C.[2]

Temple of Artemis at Sardis with the acropolis in the background

The location made Sardis a world-class trade center—one trade being the wool industry. The city was notable for the acropolis, the first temple of Artemis, and the necropolis. The city contained a large ancient synagogue. The size and central location shows the wealth and strength of the long-standing Jewish community.[3] The temple of Artemis continued after John wrote the church, but shortly afterwards began to decay. Alongside the temple a Christian church was built sometime between 300 and 400 A.D. The acropolis was formerly the site of the original city and rose eight hundred feet above the north section of Sardis. The steep rock-faced walls made the place seem impenetrable. Being virtually impregnable, the earlier location became a refuge during times of siege.

The Sardis synagogue

Former Glory

Sardis was once in the political spotlight as Persia's Asian capital, and had considerable wealth during the period of the early church. City leaders asked the Roman Senate for the honor to build a temple to Caesar, but the distinction went to Smyrna. The place represented past splendor and present decay.

The townspeople cherished past fame. Did the same mentality affect the church? Loyalty and service to Christ seemed to have been relegated to the past.

Spiritually Dead

The church appeared free of trouble without and within—there was no external threat, persecution, or internal strife—yet compromised to the point of losing authentic faith. The Christians possessed material wealth and retained an appearance of being alive but were actually dead. They no longer depended on the Holy Spirit or performed ventures of faith. Like the fig tree of Mark 11:20, they had leaves but no fruit, a non-offensive Christianity, and were not acting much like Christ.

This church is an example of churches depending on past experiences. Churches should be thankful for the past, but looking to the future. Every faith community should build its future with the same passion that created its heritage. Past history should challenge present endeavors!

Believers at Sardis established a name for themselves in the community but their lives did not measure up to God. "For the Lord sees not as man sees: man looks on the outward appearance, but the Lord looks on the heart" (1 Sam. 16:7).

Be Watchful

The church was given instructions to "wake up," or more accurately translated "be watchful." The command of watchfulness carried special meaning. The city had fallen twice to enemies from a lack of vigilance on the part of the defenders. The Greek historian Herodotus records the story of Sardis being captured by the Persian king Cyrus.

> Cyrus was besieging Sardis, and he wished to capture it with all speed, for he could not advance until Sardis was taken. He sent a message to his troops that there would be a special reward for any man who worked out a method whereby this unscalable cliff could be scaled and this untakable fortress

> taken. In his army there was a Mardian soldier called Hyeroeades. Hyeroeades gazed at the cliffs, seeking to figure out a way by which they might be stormed. He saw a Lydian [from Sardis] soldier on the battlements, and, as he watched, the Lydian accidentally dropped his helmet over the battlements, down the cliff. Hyeroeades saw this Lydian mount the battlements, pick his way down the cliffs, recover his helmet, and climb back. Hyeroaedes carefully marked in his memory the way the Lydian soldier had taken. That night he led a picked band of troops up the cliffs by that way, and when they reached the top, they found the battlements completely unguarded. The garrison never dreamed that anyone could find a way up the cliffs. They felt themselves completely safe. So Hyeroeades and his comrades entered in unopposed, and Sardis was taken. The curious thing is that the very same thing happened in the campaigns of Antiochus two hundred years later.[4]

William Barclay shares, "The Church at Sardis would hear the word *Watch!* with a memory of how necessary history had proved watchfulness to be. They would know all too well how easily the man who is too secure can find himself in disaster."[5] The church, like the city, considered themselves secure but failed to remain alert and watchful.

An Incomplete Faith

The church in Sardis was in danger of judgment. Jesus had not found them spiritually complete. The other letters showed acceptable behavior as noted by love, perseverance, truth, holiness, mission, and fervor.

Was no one coming to faith in Christ or being baptized in Sardis? Was the church simply doing religious activities? Did it love form and systems more than it loved Jesus? Were the people only born into faith and only living the faith of their parents? One thing was certain; the people in the church were consumers, not contributors. "There is a selfish Christianity which is forever looking for things from Jesus, and which forgets to ask: 'What is Jesus looking for from me?'"[6]

The church was in danger of fulfilling some of the scariest verses in the Bible. Jesus in the Sermon on the Mount said,

> Not everyone who says to me, "Lord, Lord," will enter the kingdom of heaven, but the one who does the will of my Father who is in heaven. On that day many will say to me, "Lord, Lord, did we not prophesy in your name, and cast out demons in your name, and do many mighty works in your name?" And then will I declare to them, "I never knew you; depart from me, you workers of lawlessness" (Matt. 7:21-23).

Not everyone attending church is ready for heaven; only those who bear authentic faith as a child of God.

The church in Sardis belonged to Christ in name but not heart. They could easily be labeled the first "nominal Christians." Isaiah would describe them, "They honor me with their lips, but their hearts are far from me. And their worship of me is nothing but man-made rules learned by rote" (Isa. 29:13 NLT).

The Church is called to authenticity

Whitewashed Tombs

Jesus saw firsthand the effect of *religion* without *relationship*. In speaking to religious leaders he proclaimed, "Woe to you, scribes and Pharisees, hypocrites! For you are like whitewashed tombs, which outwardly appear beautiful, but within are full of dead people's bones and all uncleanness. So you also outwardly appear righteous to others, but within you are full of hypocrisy and lawlessness" (Matt. 23:27-28).

John Stott wrote about the origin of the word hypocrite: "Originally the hupokrites was an actor, who plays a part on the stage. But the word came to be applied to any charlatan or pretender who assumes a role. Hypocrisy is make-believe; it is the 'let's pretend' of religion."[7]

Attending church to sing, pray, and listen to a message does not mean someone has a personal relationship with King Jesus. People can do perfunctory service while minds wander far from God. An authentic faith is lived out daily and is necessary for Christ followers. Are we full of the Spirit or does our life give an appearance as beautiful while inwardly full of decay?

Os Guinness tells the story of Thomas Linacre. After reading the four Gospels (Matthew, Mark, Luke, and John) for the first time in their original language, he handed them back to a priest and declared, "Either these are not the Gospels, or we are not Christians!"[8] Are we living out the message of love, truth, and holiness, or living another life?

To Repent

Sardis is the third church told to repent (the first two being Ephesus and Pergamum). They needed to make a 180-degree turn. They were told to go the opposite direction and to not return to their current condition. Jesus instructed the church to be the way it was in the beginning. If not, His appearance would be like a thief, coming at an unknown time, and with the church's works being severely judged.

Master of the Heavens

The letter to the church in Ephesus opens, "The words of him who holds the seven stars in his right hand" (Rev. 2:1). The letter to the church in Sardis begins, "The words of him who has the seven spirits of God and the seven stars" (Rev. 3:1). Genesis opens with "In the beginning, God created the heavens and the earth...And God made...the stars" (Gen. 1:1, 16). Jesus holds the key to the entrance to heaven, the Master of the heavens, the Holder of the seven stars.

To the church in Ephesus Jesus reminds them He alone can usher them safely into eternity; orthodoxy cannot save them. To the church in Sardis Jesus informs them attendance and labels are not enough. Jesus as Lord and Savior is vital for entrance into heaven. These letters give a reason for great joy. Jesus holds the seven stars. The Master and Savior controls creation and ushers us safely into eternity, if we remain faithful and authentic in our witness.

Walking With Jesus

Although the majority of the church had fully compromised its faith, a few people retained an authentic faith. A godly remnant remained. The faithful at Sardis walked with Christ dressed in white "for they are worthy." They withstood the pressure to live like the world and continued to follow Jesus. A dynamic minority of awakened and responsible believers is able by prayer, love, and witness, to restore a dying Church and bring her back to life.

Plod On

William Carey, a globally-minded Christian from the 1700s, committed himself to living and working in India. One of his more famous quotes is, "Expect great things from God. Attempt great things for God."

As an old man, he talked to his nephew about the possibility of someone writing about his life. He said, "If he gives me credit for being a plodder, he will describe me justly. Anything beyond this will be too much. I can plod. I can persevere in any definite pursuit. To this I owe everything."[9] Part of following Jesus involves plodding on as an authentic Christian for an entire lifetime.

The Spirit of God

The greatest gift believers are given and can ever receive is the Spirit of God. "He enters our human personality and changes us from within. He fills us with love, joy, and peace. He subdues our passions and transforms our characters into the likeness of Christ. Today there is no manmade temple in which God dwells. Instead, his temple is his people. He inhabits both the individual believer and the Christian community."[10]

When Jesus admonishes the church in Sardis to remember, He is calling them back to life in the Spirit. Stott shares, "It is the Holy Spirit who can breathe life into our formal worship and who can animate our dead works until they pulsate with life. He can rescue a dying church and make it a living force in the community. Let him once fill us with his vital presence, and our work, worship, and witness will all be marvelously transformed."[11]

Scripture instructs us to pray in the Spirit (Jude 20), preach in the Spirit (1 Thess. 1:5), worship in the Spirit (John 4:24; Phil. 3:3), live in the Spirit, and walk in the Spirit (Gal. 5:16, 25). The Spirit of God brings life where there is death. Believers are to be continually filled with the Holy Spirit (Eph. 5:18).

More than simply dwelling within, does He fill us? We may possess Him, but does He possess us? "If we would but submit to the authority of the Spirit, 'keep in step with the Spirit' (Gal. 5:25), and continuously seek the Spirit's fullness, our Christian life would be transformed and our church life revolutionized."[12]

The Promise

Greek cities in the ancient world maintained a list of male citizens in a public register. When a citizen was condemned for committing a crime, he lost citizenship and had his name erased from the register. One of the promises of Jesus is the victor's name not being erased from the Book of Life.[13] If followers of Jesus turn back to authentic faith, they have the promise of heavenly white robes, their names remaining in the Book of Life, and Jesus acknowledging them before God and the angels. Faithfulness during present-day trials is rewarded beyond measure in the life to come.

Mission Value: Authentic Contextualization

Jesus contextualizes the message in these seven letters. He made them all meaningful to their audience and culture. The seven churches received different comments, just as He desires to speak a unique word to everyone. He has a special message for every congregation. He knows exactly what is going on in every church—their successes, failures, victories, problems, challenges, and difficulties. To the church in Sardis, he says, "Be watchful." To Thyatira, the place of cultic worship for Apollo Tyrimnos, a son of Zeus, Jesus starts His message as the resurrected Christ, the true Son of God. To the church in Pergamum, Jesus is described with "the sharp, two-edged sword." In a city where the proconsul was granted the "right of the sword," the power to execute, the sovereign Christ reminds the threatened congregation the ultimate power of life and death belongs to God.

Presenting the message of Jesus in ways people can understand is important. Paul wrote to the Corinthians, "I try to find common ground with everyone, doing everything I can to save some" (1 Cor. 9:22 NLT). Tim Keller talks about the Pauline method in *Center Church*. "Paul varies his use of emotion and reason, his vocabulary, his introductions and conclusions, his figures of speech and illustrations, his identification of the audience's concerns, hopes, and needs. In every case, he adapts his gospel presentation to his hearers."[14]

John in his Gospel wrote, "In the beginning, was the Word" (1:1). This one statement spoke to both Greek and Hebrew. The Greeks desire for wisdom, insight, and understanding was summed up in the Word, a complete understanding of the spiritual and physical world, of the human soul, and life after death. All these questions are answered in Jesus.

For the Hebrew, the totality of the Old Testament begins with "in the beginning." John is announcing a new beginning in Jesus the Messiah. The Hebrew concept of law, sacred words, morality, justice, and righteousness are found in Jesus.

Keller describes contextualization as keeping "a balance between affirming and confronting culture."[15] Every culture is "a mixed bag of good and bad elements."[16] Affirming qualities found in the Bible while confronting those that challenge the Truth is important. In attempting to reach different cultures,

> Our stance toward every human culture should be one of critical enjoyment and an appropriate wariness. Yes, we should enjoy the insights and the creativity of other peoples and cultures. We should recognize and celebrate expressions of justice, wisdom, truth, and beauty in every culture. But we approach every culture with awareness that it has been distorted by sin and in particular, the sin of idolatry. All cultures contain elements of darkness and light.[17]

Paul contextualizes by revealing the fatal contradictions and underlying idolatry within different cultures and then points them to the resolution found only in Christ.[18]

Jesus answers every question any human can possibly ask. Out of love God sent one pure Light into a world of darkness. Everyone needs to fix their eyes on Him and come to the Father. We live in a dark world, aimlessly wandering and lost, in a place void of light. God revealed himself in Jesus and longs for everyone to be His child. He wants to adopt and bring us home. He desires to embrace everyone. Make the decision to embrace Him. Accept Jesus as Lord and believe in His resurrection.

Hindus work to appease the wrath of the gods. Jesus hung on a cross and consumed the wrath of God for all mankind. David Platt writes,

> "What happened at the Cross was not primarily about nails being thrust into Jesus' hands and feet but about the wrath due your sin and my sin being thrust upon his soul. In that holy moment, all the righteous wrath and justice of God due us came rushing down like a torrent on Christ himself… At the Cross, Christ drank the full cup of the wrath of God, and when he had downed the last drop, he turned the cup over and cried out, 'It is finished.'"[19]

Buddhists desire peace with God. Jesus came to reconcile humanity to God, bringing peace. "The just and loving Creator of the universe has looked upon hopelessly sinful people and sent his Son, God in the flesh, to bear his wrath against sin on the cross and to show his power over sin in the Resurrection so that all who trust in him will be reconciled to God forever."[20]

Muslims want to go to heaven. Jesus came with the assurance that believing in Him leads to life everlasting. No one has to guess about eternity when he or she puts faith in Christ.

Contextually pointing people to Jesus is critical. Jesus is the answer.

Keller lays out a three-part process of contextualizing. "Entering the culture, challenging the culture, and then appealing to the listeners… The first task of contextualization is to immerse yourself in the questions, hopes, and beliefs of the culture so you can give a biblical, gospel-centered response to its questions."[21] Spending time with people in their culture is vital for proper contextualization. This is often simple for people living in familiar surroundings but a challenge for those moving from a rural to an urban setting, or from one country to another.

The next task involves challenging the culture. Affirming beliefs that align or are neutral to Christian beliefs and using them to bridge beliefs that go against the message of Jesus.

The final task is appealing to the listener. "We show our listeners that the plotlines of their lives can only find a resolution, a 'happy ending,' in Jesus."[22] This happens because "the Bible has enough diversity to enable us to connect its message to any baseline cultural narrative on the face of the earth."[23]

The Message

Was your faith greater in the past? Are you building the future with the same Spirit-filled passion that initially established your walk with the Lord?

Have authentic faith. Be unwilling to adopt the patterns of the world. The needs of the world are so great that we cannot afford to dabble in religion or be insincere in our relationship with God.[24]

Living an Authentic Faith

About a year after receiving word from Stan about his diagnosis, my family was visiting the ancient sites of the seven churches in Turkey. An email arrived that shared Stan had passed away. The day we visited the site of Sardis, the church called to authenticity, Stan went to his heavenly home.

Stan received permission to be buried in the Euphrates Valley in the Dark Canyon region in an old Christian graveyard. No one has been buried at this site in 100 years because Christians no longer live in the area. But Jesus was preached at Stan's memorial service in Istanbul and at the burial site in the Dark Canyon. He lived a life of authenticity, showing Turkish friends hope for the future even when facing death.

The Challenge

Return to authentic faith and display God to the world. Be continually filled with the Spirit, manifesting resurrection power! The reward is great—eternity with Jesus among people from every nation, tribe, and language. Stan lived for Jesus in life and death. His challenge for us is, "There is more. Regardless of where you're at right now, God wants to do more with you."[25]

Small Group Discussion Starters

1. Follow-up from previous discussion: Can anyone remember the five steps for renewing your mind (realize, recognize, renounce, release, renewal)? Did anyone work through this process of "active holiness" this week? Would anyone be willing to share an area of life that you surrendered to Jesus?
2. What area of your life is not measuring up to God's standards?
3. What kind of active contribution are you making to your church?
4. How are you learning to daily walk in the Spirit?
5. What steps are you taking to build your future with the same Spirit-filled passion with which you began?

As a group hold each other accountable to living authentic lives. Ask the Holy Spirit to reveal areas in your life not measuring up to His standard. Learn to walk in the Spirit and build your future with passion.

Chapter Eight

CALLED TO MISSION

"Mission was not made for the church; the church was made for mission— God's mission."
–Chris Wright

"I am not going to be able to come back and teach this year." Not an email anyone wants to receive a few weeks before an international school is scheduled to start. And especially not while on vacation with the family. The email came from the middle school English teacher saying she would not be returning in August. Out of frustration I prayed, "Well, God, this school is not my school. It's not the superintendent's school. It's yours, and you need a teacher." The next day I received an email from one of our teachers letting me know he and his wife met a girl with an English degree interested in working at the school. God found a teacher for His school.

Hudson Taylor made the statement, "God isn't looking for people of great faith, but for individuals ready to follow Him."[1] Jenni, the girl with the English degree, was ready to follow Jesus to Jerusalem. Are you ready to follow Jesus into His mission? The letter to the church in Philadelphia reveals that we have been called to mission.

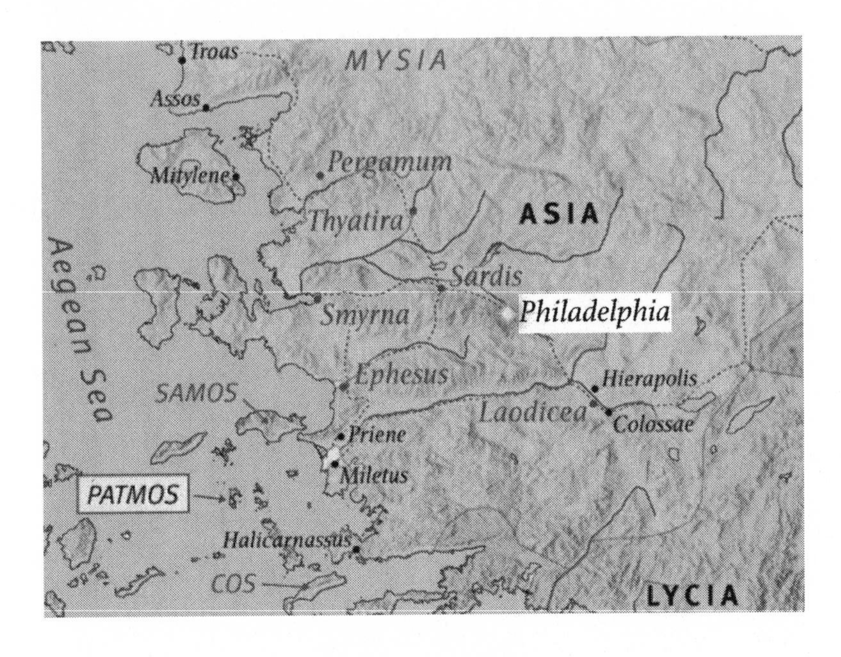

Revelation 3:7-13

"And to the angel of the church in Philadelphia write: 'The words of the holy one, the true one, who has the key of David, who opens and no one will shut, who shuts and no one opens.'

'I know your works. Behold, I have set before you an open door, which no one is able to shut. I know that you have but little power, and yet you have kept my word and have not denied my name. Behold, I will make those of the synagogue of Satan who say that they are Jews and are not, but lie—behold, I will make them come and bow down before your feet, and they will learn that I have loved you. Because you have kept my word about patient endurance, I will keep you from the hour of trial that is coming on the whole world, to try those who dwell on the earth. I am coming soon. Hold fast what you have, so that no one may seize your crown. The one who conquers, I will make him a pillar in the temple of my God. Never shall he go out of it, and I will write on him the name of my God, and the name of the city of my God, the new Jerusalem, which comes down from my God out of heaven, and my own new name. He who has an ear, let him hear what the Spirit says to the churches.'"

Ancient Philadelphia

Twenty-five miles southeast of Sardis, along the Hermus River valley, sits the high plateau city of Philadelphia. Pergamenian king Attalus II, who the Romans tried to turn against his brother Eumenes II, established the city. Attalus remained loyal and gained the nickname "Philadelphus" because of a deep-seeded love for his brother. Along with textile and leather industries, a vine-growing area to the northeast contributed greatly to the city's prosperity.

Philadelphia rested along one of the great travel routes of the world, the highway leading from Europe to the East.[2] Strategically located on the trade routes to Mysia, Lydia, and Phrygia, the city earned the title "gateway to the East," the entryway from one continent to another. Philadelphia disseminated Greek culture and language into far distant regions. The city was also a pagan worship center, having so many gods and temples it was referred to as "little Athens."

A Faithful Church

The letter to Philadelphia does not contain disapproval or reproach, but addresses a church keeping the faith. Churches can have a strong testimony and a vibrant witness. Not every church experiences trouble. Jesus addresses the church, "I know that you have but little power, and yet you have kept my word and have not denied my name" (Rev. 3:8). Followers of Jesus must be obedient in action and fearless in witness.

Long after the surrounding country of Turkey succumbed to Muslim control, Philadelphia was a Christian community until 1392. Visiting the ruins of the church in Philadelphia was a somber experience, the smallest site of the seven churches. All that remained were the broken ruins and pillars of the Church of St. John the Theologian. Christian sarcophaguses (stone coffins) were scattered on the grounds. Philadelphia was a faithful church.

Church of St. John the Theologian in Philadelphia

Holy, True & Authentic

Jesus is addressed as the holy and true One. He is real and genuine, calling His Church to holiness, truth, and authenticity. Real and genuine truth is found in Him.

Order Matters

The letters to the Asian churches were arranged in the book of Revelation according to a mail delivery route. A circular roadway went north past Ephesus through Smyrna to Pergamum, turned east and south toward Thyatira and Sardis, and then east to Philadelphia before heading south again to Laodicea.

Although the letters followed a postal route, did the order also portray following Jesus and engaging in mission? As earlier stated by A. W. Tozer, the Church must first be worthy to spread the message of Jesus. To be involved in mission, a person needs to love well, embrace suffering, walk in truth and holiness, and maintain an authentic faith. How a person embraces these components determines his or her long-term service and effectiveness in mission.

Preparing for battle includes wilderness experiences and genuine community where people sharpen their steel (love, suffering, truth, holiness, authenticity, mission, and fervor). To successfully walk through an open door for mission, a person must be ready.

An Open Door

The church in Philadelphia had an open door. They had the geographical ability to widely spread the message of Jesus everywhere. When addressing mission, Paul mentioned open doors on a couple of occasions (2 Cor. 2:12; Col. 4:3). He wrote the Corinthian church of his plans to stay in Ephesus until the Feast of Weeks (Pentecost) and declared, "There is a wide-open door for a great work here" (1 Cor. 16:9 NLT).

The Church is called to mission

One Door Opens Another

After working with the international school in Sudan, we returned to the U. S. for the birth of our daughter. Shortly after bringing her home, friends told us about the school in Jerusalem. The work with the school in Sudan led us to Jerusalem. Often a person must be willing to walk through one door to find the next. We had to move from Point A to Point B to discover the ultimate Point C. Point B, Sudan, was our wilderness experience but was absolutely necessary to find success in Point C, Jerusalem. Had we not embraced Jesus in the wilderness, we would not have walked through the Jerusalem door.

A Doorway to Divine Fellowship

The church in Philadelphia had an open door for relationship with Jesus and living in His Kingdom. Although local believers were possibly kicked out of the local synagogue, Jesus is described as "the one who has the key of David." He is the door into divine fellowship. An identity with Jesus may close some doors, but obeying God and not denying Jesus gains the open door of divine fellowship. Adversaries might try to close doors but they cannot succeed. When ambitions and motivations are right, we can expect God's help. No earthly power can stand against Him (Rom. 8:31).

The Key

Jesus opens the door that no one can shut because He holds the key. The door serves as a symbol of opportunity for mission and the key serves as a symbol for Christ's authority.

When Jesus talks of building His Church, he tells Peter he will be given the keys of the kingdom. Peter, walking in the authority of Christ, uses those keys to take the message of Jesus to Jews on the day of Pentecost (Acts 2:14-41), to Samaritans (8:14-17), and to Gentiles (10:44-48).

This authority has been passed on to those who call Him Lord. Before sending out His followers with the message of hope and love, Jesus declares, "I have given you authority over all the power of the enemy, and you can walk among snakes and scorpions and crush them. Nothing will injure you" (Luke 10:19 NLT). As followers of the One who holds the key, we can engage in mission with the confidence He goes before us. We partner in building His Church and have been granted His authority to do it.

Jesus' final words before ascending to heaven were, "All authority in heaven and on earth has been given to me. Go therefore and make disciples of all nations, baptizing them in the name of the Father and of the Son and of the Holy Spirit, teaching them to observe all that I have commanded you. And behold, I am with you always, to the end of the age" (Matt. 28:18-20). Every church should have a vision for mission, locally and globally.

Vision Casting

This chapter's opening quote from Chris Wright emphasizes the Church is made for mission. Does your church reflect this? If not, create a picture of what this should look like.

Andy Stanley shares with church leaders, "Your responsibility is to make the people in your church discontent with where they are by painting a compelling picture of where they could be."[3] This is difficult if a church falls in love with a particular model, despite the intended mission. The church has been called to mission, not models. "When a *church* fails to distinguish between its current *model* and the *mission* to which it has been called and mistakenly fossilizes around its *model*, that church sets itself up for decline."[4] Continued growth requires (1) fulfilling the mission of the Church, namely making disciples, and (2) having a vision, model, and program that supports the mission where the church is located and beyond (Acts 1:8).

How does a church develop a vision, based on mission, that affects its model and programs? Start by asking questions. "Asking the right questions (and asking them over and over) will ensure that the vision of your church remains paramount while your programming remains subservient."[5] Stanley offers several questions:[6]

- Do our members and attendees know why we exist?
- What have we fallen in love with that's not as effective as it used to be?
- What are we promoting that we wish we didn't have to personally attend?
- Is there a natural relationship between what we measure and our mission?
- Is there a natural relationship between what we celebrate and our mission?
- If our church suddenly ceased to exist, would our community miss us?

Asking questions will drive models and programs to align with mission and vision. But remember, the Spirit of God leads the Church. An ear to hear what the Spirit says is vital for a mission and vision to reflect the Church Jesus desires to build.

John Lindell, the lead pastor of James River Church, takes time every year to both celebrate God's victories in the previous year and to share with the church how the Spirit is speaking for the coming year. Vision Sunday has become an integral part of motivating the entire church to come together and unite with common mission and vision for the future.

Why does a church need a vision for a preferred future? Vision is critical for facing mission. David had vision when he faced Goliath. Samuel the prophet already anointed him as the next King of Israel (1 Sam. 16:13). When he faced Goliath, he knew God would go before him to complete the task. A church needs solid missional vision to engage in God's work and take down the God-mocking giants of the day. A church vision should first emphasize a longing for Jesus and then a yearning to see His name made famous to the ends of the earth.

Lo and Go

John York stated there is no "go" without "lo," the "lo, I am with you always." First, we are called to Jesus, He is with us always, and we are with Him. Then we go to the uttermost parts and pressures of the world.[7] There is a door for mission open for every follower of Christ. All Christians should be mission-minded. The door is open, but the choice to engage in God's mission is ours.

The Mission of God

God has an eternal purpose for His whole creation. While God came to save individual people, His grace does not revolve around one person's needs. Mission flows from the purposes of God, a "committed participation as God's people, at God's invitation and command, in God's own mission with the history of God's world for the redemption of God's creation."[8]

A call has been extended to the Church for a global outreach of a global people from a global God.[9] It is God's story and we are participants in it.[10] "It is not so much the case that God has a mission for his church in the world, as that God has a church for his mission in the world."[11]

What is the mission of God? Peace (*shalom*) in community in the presence of God. Our picture of eternity reflects this, "I looked, and behold, a great multitude that no one could number, from every nation, from all tribes and peoples and languages, standing before the throne and before the Lamb, clothed in white robes, with palm branches in their hands, and crying out with a loud voice, 'Salvation belongs to our God who sits on the throne, and to the Lamb'" (Rev. 7:9-10)! Shortly after recording the letters to the seven churches, John records this vision, multitudes of people abiding together in peace before the throne.

A Mission of Peace

Genesis records man and woman created in perfect shalom with God (Gen. 1 & 2). Adam and Eve had community with God and each other, as well as shalom with all creation. John records a vision of shalom represented around the throne room of God by every people group. Humanity starts and ends in peace. Paul records Jesus came to establish peace.

> Don't forget that you Gentiles used to be outsiders. You were called "uncircumcised heathens" by the Jews, who were proud of their circumcision, even though it affected only their bodies and not their hearts. In those days you were living apart from Christ. You were excluded from citizenship among the people of Israel, and you did not know the covenant promises God had made to them. You lived in this world without God and without hope. But now you have been united with Christ Jesus. Once you were far away from God, but now you have been brought near to him through the blood of Christ.
>
> For Christ himself has brought peace to us. He united Jews and Gentiles into one people when, in his own body on the cross, he broke down the wall of hostility that separated us. He did this by ending the system of law with its commandments and regulations. He made peace between Jews and Gentiles by creating in himself one new people from the two groups. Together as one body, Christ reconciled both groups to God by means of his death on the cross, and our hostility toward each other was put to death.
>
> He brought this Good News of peace to you Gentiles who were far away from him, and peace to the Jews who were near. Now all of us can come to the Father through the same

> Holy Spirit because of what Christ has done for us (Eph. 2:11-18 NLT).

Jesus brought shalom. His birth came with the glorious announcement, "peace on earth" (Luke 2:14). Jesus was the divine peacemaker, caring for both Jew and Gentile. He understood the sun rises and rain falls on all mankind (Matt. 5:45). He lived at a time described as the "Pax Romana" or Roman peace. The Roman Empire established and maintained peace through military might. Jesus, however, referred to a peace that makes a person whole, not simply the absence of war.

Shalom is described as a state of mind, inward soundness, and wellbeing. People often tell me they pray for the peace of Jerusalem. I remind them to pray for the wellbeing of all Jerusalem's inhabitants—Jews, Palestinians, Armenians, secular Israelis, Druze, Samaritans, Russians, Europeans, all who walk its streets and call it home.

Humanity started in peace and ends in peace, and Jesus models peace in His mission, a mission the Church is to continue. Part of engaging in the mission of Jesus is working toward peace among all humanity until the glorious day when Jesus returns and establishes His final peace.

The Mission of Jesus

Choosing to walk through the door of mission means to engage in the mission of Jesus. His mission is an active one. Os Guinness writes about the mission of the church and points out, "Faithful presence is not enough. It is merely the beginning."[12]

Jesus gives His inaugural address in the synagogue at Nazareth by reading from Isaiah, "The Spirit of the Lord is upon me, because he has anointed me to proclaim good news to the poor. He has sent me to proclaim liberty to the captives and recovering of sight to the blind, to set at liberty those who are oppressed, to proclaim the year of the Lord's favor" (Luke 4:18-19). He then delivers a profoundly short message, "Today this Scripture has been fulfilled in your hearing" (v. 21).

The Spirit of the Lord was upon Jesus. He is the anointed One of God. He announces the dawning of the Messianic age; an event was taking place before the people's eyes. He came to proclaim good news, show compassion (recovery of sight to the blind), and provide justice advocacy (liberty to the captives and oppressed).[13] Jesus was not merely present in the world. He was intensely active. He taught truth, healed diseases, cast out evil spirits, drove out corruption, raised the dead, confronted hypocrisy, and willingly laid down His life on the cross.[14]

Like Him we must actively proclaim the life, death, and resurrection of Jesus, engage in justice advocacy for the oppressed, and show compassion to the needs of others. Fulfilling His mission may lead to suffering and persecution. This was the case for the church in Philadelphia. But Jesus lifted them up.

A Humbling Message

"I will force those who belong to Satan's synagogue…to come and bow down at your feet. They will acknowledge that you are the ones I love." When believers are verbally attacked and denounced by others, those people will someday be humbled and acknowledge Jesus as the true Messiah (Rom. 14:11).

The Promise

Philadelphia often experienced devastating earthquakes, causing people to flee and set-up temporary housing in rural areas. The promise of permanence within the New Jerusalem held a special meaning, one of safety. Residents would no longer need to fear disaster. Nothing could separate them from the love of God.

Paul had a similar confidence.

> And I am convinced that nothing can ever separate us from God's love. Neither death nor life, neither angels nor demons, neither our fears for today nor our worries about tomorrow—not even the powers of hell can separate us from God's love. No power in the sky above or in the earth below—indeed, nothing in all creation will ever be able to separate us from the love of God that is revealed in Christ Jesus our Lord (Rom. 8:38-39 NLT).

In Philadelphia, when a man served the state well, the city built a pillar in one of the temples as a memorial with his name inscribed on it.[15] Jesus promises overcomers, "The one who conquers, I will make him a pillar in the temple of my God. Never shall he go out of it" (Rev. 3:12). His followers are forever honored in the house of God.

The faithful will have the name of God written on them (Rev. 3:12). A follower of Jesus should be living in such a way that others can see they are the property of God. Jesus assures those who valiantly walk through open doors, waging war against the powers of evil, and are victorious in the fight, that they will forever belong to God.

In a city known for various games and festivals, a promised crown was especially appropriate. Perseverance would lead to a victorious crown. Jesus promises the faithful belong to God, are citizens of the New Jerusalem, and maintain a special relationship with Him.

A Pillar

Individuals who invest in the wellbeing of others in a town are sometimes labeled "a pillar in the community." A first-century tradition has become a commonly used phrase in our day. A pillar's function is to support and uphold important structures. There are many within the Church serving well, yet there are others who concern themselves only with what they can get. Some desire to support the Church while others want to be supported. We gain from church only what we invest.

A community of faith is meant to serve one another. "Bear one another's burdens, and so fulfill the law of Christ. For if anyone thinks he is something, when he is nothing, he deceives himself. But let each one test his own work, and then his reason to boast will be in himself alone and not in his neighbor. For each will have to bear his own load" (Gal. 6:2-5).

Which is it? Bear one another's burdens, or bear your own load? Is it both? The "I" culture mentioned earlier places emphasis on individuals. Yet biblically functioning communities attempt to care for their own needs while supporting others. If the load is backpack size, carry it yourself. But a trunk requires help—ask for help when needed. A pillar in the church supports members and ministries. Learn to be a contributor more than a consumer. The church on a mission needs pillars.

Mission Value: Missional Church

Upon return to England after thirty years of working in India, Lesslie Newbigin, a church pillar, realized the Church was working hard to attract people but falling short of going on mission to reach them.[16] Followers of Jesus were not fulfilling the mandate recorded by John, "As the Father has sent me, even so I am sending you" (John 20:21).

Mission refers to all God is doing and all He calls the Church to do in cooperation with Him. Mission involved sending His Son and now involves sending His Church. The Church is more than an organization providing spiritual merchandise and attractive programs. The Church is missional. "God's people are a sign to the world of who God is."[17] Jesus embodies the mission, the Holy Spirit empowers the mission, the Church is the instrument of mission, and the culture is the context of mission.[18]

A missional church is "on mission," meaning "being intentional and deliberate about reaching others."[19] The emphasis is not redoing programs but rediscovering the mission of inviting people to a new way of life. Mission is not an action or program but the essence of purpose pervading all the church.[20] Missional people live godly before a watching world. They exhibit the fruit of the Spirit, expressing love, joy, peace, patience, kindness, goodness, and self control. They walk in truth and holiness, have authentic love for others, engage in justice advocacy, care for the poor, and talk about Jesus. "A church becomes missional when it remains faithful to the gospel and simultaneously seeks to contextualize the gospel (to the degree it can) so the gospel engages the hearers and transforms their worldview."[21] A contextual presentation of the message of Jesus is important to the missional church.

Missional engagement is different for every location. A church must enter the local community, live with people, and listen to their stories. It must then discover what God is doing in the people's midst. Get outside the walls of the church and find out what is happening among the people in a neighborhood. Enter people's lives, sit at their tables, and listen to what the Spirit is doing.[22] Believers should be on mission everyday with every interaction.

The mission of God is global. While reaching neighbors, it is vital to remember those with little or no access to the message of Jesus. They need to be reached. Being missional in North America "cannot be at the expense of the truly unreached and least-reached in the frontier mission sense."[23] The Western church is to be missional where they are located *and* motivated to places having no access and few resources in every part of the world. Anything less is tragic.[24]

Mission calls people to a journey bigger than themselves, having a radically different vision of the world. The purposes of God are discovered by leaving behind security. Life is found by losing it (Matt. 10:39).

The Message

What motivates you? Are you pursuing opportunities to serve in the Kingdom? Are you engaging in the mission of Jesus, proclaiming the Good News? Are you working to establish peace? Are you engaging in justice advocacy for the oppressed? Are you doing acts of compassion that meet the needs of others?

Expect His help, but also expect criticism. Not everyone is happy when you successfully represent Jesus.

An Urgent Need

John Stott accurately prescribes the Church as urgently needing believers of profound zeal, willing to count all things loss for God's glory and willing to hazard life, comfort, career, and reputation for Him. Open doors are many, but few are going through them. "He sets before us the open doors of salvation and of service. He bids us go in through the one to receive salvation and out through the other to give service."[25]

Think of Jesus' call as two-fold. First "come and see," and then "go and die." Jesus says come and see the pearl of great price, a hidden treasure. Then go give everything you have for it. Dietrich Bonhoeffer claims, "When Christ calls a man, He bids him come and die."[26]

The Challenge

Pursue open doors given by God. Engage in the global mission of proclamation, justice advocacy, peacemaking, and compassion. Seek opportunities to make disciples and advance His kingdom, locally and globally.

Small Group Discussion Starters

1. Follow-up from previous discussion: What did you do to "freshen" up your faith this past week? In what ways did you display an authentic love of God and neighbor to those around you?

2. What doors have you walked through in the past in response to fulfilling God's mission?
3. What God-given opportunities are open to you that you are hesitant to pursue?
4. How can you engage in the mission of Jesus in your home, neighborhood, workplace, and church (proclamation, justice advocacy, peacemaking, and acts of compassion)?
5. How are you engaging in the global mission of God where little or no access is available? Where is the mission taking you (literally and/or figuratively)?

As a group hold each other accountable to engage in the mission of God. Pray and ask God to reveal open doors and give you strength to walk through them. Ask for discernment on how to share His message, establish peace, engage in justice advocacy, and meet the needs of others.

Chapter Nine

CALLED TO FERVOR

John Wesley was asked how he attracted great crowds.
He replied: "I set myself on fire, and the people come to see me burn."

There exists a parable of an older man named Arthur who absolutely loved Jesus. One day his grandson visited his home in the country and while sitting on his porch, asked his grandfather why he loved Jesus so much.

Arthur motioned to his dog Buster and shared that Buster had chased a rabbit a few days before. Other dogs joined him, but after a while they gave up the chase. Buster, though, continued pursuing the rabbit. Arthur asked his grandson if he knew why Buster never gave up. His grandson didn't know. He explained that Buster was the only one who actually saw the rabbit. Knowing the rabbit was there kept Buster in the race.

Arthur's experience with Jesus kept the fervor alive. With spiritual sight he saw Jesus and never lost the fervor of fresh faith.

In each of the seven letters, Jesus emphasizes a different trait characterizing true and living churches. Ephesus is urged to return to its first love, while Smyrna is encouraged to endure suffering and hardship. Pergamum is to champion truth in the midst of error, and Thyatira is to embrace holiness in the midst of evil. Sardis needed to display an authentic and genuine faith. Philadelphia had a mission to fulfill.[1] The final letter to the church in Laodicea stresses spiritual fervor.

Revelation 3:14-22

"And to the angel of the church in Laodicea write: 'The words of the Amen, the faithful and true witness, the beginning of God's creation.'

'I know your works: you are neither cold nor hot. Would that you were either cold or hot! So, because you are lukewarm, and neither hot nor cold, I will spit you out of my mouth. For you say, I am rich, I have prospered, and I need nothing, not realizing that you are wretched, pitiable, poor, blind, and naked. I counsel you to buy from me gold refined by fire, so that you may be rich, and white garments so that you may clothe yourself and the shame of your nakedness may not be seen, and salve to anoint your eyes, so that you may see. Those whom I love, I reprove and discipline, so be zealous and repent. Behold, I stand at the door and knock. If anyone hears my voice and opens the door, I will come in to him and eat with him, and he with me. The one who conquers, I will grant him to sit with me on my throne, as I also conquered and sat down with my Father on his throne. He who has an ear, let him hear what the Spirit says to the churches.'"

Colonnaded street in Laodicea

Ancient Laodicea

Laodicea was forty-five miles southeast of Philadelphia and one hundred miles due east of Ephesus. The Roman road stretching inland to Asia from Ephesus ran straight through the city, making Laodicea an important trade and communication center.

Laodicea's position made her one of the richest commercial centers of the ancient world. The Lycus valley provided good grazing for sheep with in-demand soft black wool.

Prosperity also brought the banking industry to Laodicea. The town was wealthy enough to not need public assistance. Following a devastating earthquake in AD 60 the city was rebuilt without financial help from Rome.

The city also had a school of medicine. They manufactured and distributed a special ointment called "Phrygian powder," famous for curing eye defects.

A Pauline Church

The church was possibly founded by Epaphras (Col. 4:12) when Paul was spending time at Ephesus (Acts 19:10). It does not appear that Paul visited the church, although the letter to Colossians was read to the church in Laodicea (Col. 4:16).

A Stern Letter

Jesus sends the Laodicean church a harsh letter, containing correction and no praise. The Laodiceans had put their trust in wealth, luxury, and health. The letter served as a warning to those putting trust in material things and leaving God out.[2]

A Lukewarm Church

Jesus claims the church in Laodicea was neither hot nor cold. When it comes to beverages, people prefer one or the other. I like hot coffee in the morning and prefer cold water after exercise. Lukewarm is never great.

Water in Laodicea came via an aqueduct, not near a natural source, and often arrived lukewarm. Compared to the hot medicinal waters of nearby Hierapolis and the mountainous snow-fed cold waters of neighboring Colossae, the waters of Laodicea lacked desirability.

The church was not spiritually refreshing for the weary or those needing healing. Without spiritual fervor the church was totally ineffective. It was distasteful to the Lord. The church became complacent and lacked a sense of urgency. It was drifting rather than driving. William Barclay pointed out the church was "condemned because she preferred a respectable morality to a passionate religion."[3]

The word translated "hot" refers to a boiling point. An inner spiritual fire is in constant danger of dying and needs to be poked, fed, and fanned into flame.[4] Paul instructed the Christians in Rome to be "fervent in spirit" (Rom. 12:11).

The Church is called to fervor

Christians Aflame

The church needs courageous men and women with an inexhaustible fire in their bones for the things of God. How many pray in Augustinian fashion, "Revive the church, O Lord, beginning with me?"

If Jesus is true, if He is the Son of God come in human form to die for sin and be raised from the dead, if Christmas, Good Friday, and Easter are more than meaningless anniversaries, then nothing less than wholehearted commitment to Christ will do—putting Him first, seeking His glory, and obeying His will.[5]

Do you have a zeal, fervor, fire, and passion for the things of God? Do fervor, perseverance, truth, holiness, authenticity, and mission motivate you?

A Lack of Urgency

A story is told of three demons leaving hell to fill the earth with evil. Before leaving, they each told Satan their plan. One said, "I will tell men there is no God." "That," said Satan, "will not do. In their heart of hearts they know He exists." "I will tell men," said the second, "there is no hell." "That," said Satan, "is hopeless. Even in life they have experienced the pangs of hell." "I will tell men," said the third, "there is no hurry." "Go," said Satan, "you will ruin them by the millions."[6]

A loss of fervor leads to complacency in mission. If the church forgets people are perishing everyday without the saving knowledge of Jesus, she loses.

An Affluent Church

The affluent Laodicean church was unaware of her wretched, miserable, poor, blind, and naked condition. The people interpreted material wealth as blessing and like the farmer in Jesus' parable were eating, drinking, and living merrily, thinking many good things were laid up for years to come (Luke 12:19). They felt secure in material attainment, choosing comfort over Christ. They had little to offer of spiritual value and were desperately in need of restoration.

The city and church were so financially secure they believed there was no need for help from God or man. As already mentioned, an earthquake in AD 60 devastated the whole region and Laodicea was promptly rebuilt without help from Rome.[7] Jesus describes them as beggars despite their banks, naked despite their clothing industry, and blind despite their eye powders. Although the city could manage without public aid, they could not manage without King Jesus.

The Pride of the City

Laodicea prided itself on financial wealth, an extensive textile industry, and an eye salve exported around the world. This letter shows Jesus provides the church counsel, "I counsel you to…" (Rev. 3:18). Christians serve a God willing to personally speak truth in love.

Jesus instructs the church to buy gold refined in fire, a gold having passed through the Refiner's fire and found trustworthy. They were spiritually poor, yet Christ had heavenly gold.

In contrast to the black woolen fabric manufactured in the city, the Laodiceans also needed white clothes to cover shameful nakedness. They were vainly concerned about what they wore and neglected their spiritual state. They were spiritually naked, yet Christ had heavenly clothes.

Spiritual shortcomings were rooted in spiritual blindness. The producers of eye salve needed to recognize a lack of vision—it was something the local medicine could not cure. They were spiritually blind, yet Christ had heavenly eye salve. The counsel of Jesus was much needed to spiritually naked and blind beggars.[8]

Heaven on Earth

Some believe if people have better pay, working conditions, and health care, heaven can be experienced on earth. Yet Jesus defines a blessed life differently in Matthew 5:3-10 (NLT):

- God blesses those who are poor and realize their need for him, for the Kingdom of Heaven is theirs.
- God blesses those who mourn, for they will be comforted.

- God blesses those who are humble, for they will inherit the whole earth.
- God blesses those who hunger and thirst for justice, for they will be satisfied.
- God blesses those who are merciful, for they will be shown mercy.
- God blesses those whose hearts are pure, for they will see God.
- God blesses those who work for peace, for they will be called the children of God.
- God blesses those who are persecuted for doing right, for the Kingdom of Heaven is theirs.

In other words, heaven is experienced on earth when people realize a deep need for God, mourn over sin, become right with God, are compassionate and moved toward action, pursue peace with others, and embrace hardship.

Transforming Culture

The aim of Christianity is not so much to change conditions as to change people. If people change, their conditions are transformed.[9] Sociologist Robert Woodberry after a decade of research on the effects of Christians working in cross-cultural settings wrote, "Areas where [expat Christians] had a significant presence in the past are on average more economically developed today, with comparatively better health, lower infant mortality, lower corruption, greater literacy, higher educational attainment (especially for women), and more robust membership in nongovernmental associations."[10]

John Piper, commenting on Woodberry's article, points out "the way to achieve the greatest social and cultural transformation is not to focus on social and cultural transformation, but on the [proclamation of the message of Jesus], the forgiveness of sins and the hope of eternal life."[11] Christians better the world not by focusing on changing the world, but by placing faith in Jesus.

If the tree is good, so is its fruit (Matt. 12:33). If a person decides to follow Jesus, he or she has the capacity to bear honorable qualities. A renewing of the mind leads to positive transformation and change. The focus should be faith in Jesus and reflection of His character. Our aim should always be advancing the kingdom of God rather than recreating culture.[12]

Prosperity and Safety

Two things can cause a lukewarm existence—prosperity and lack of persecution. The Laodicean church had money but was not troubled by false teaching or civil unrest. The church became self-satisfied, self-deceived, and self-righteous. "Perhaps none of the seven letters is more appropriate to the church at the beginning of the 21st century than this. It describes vividly the respectable, nominal, rather sentimental, skin-deep religiosity which is so widespread among us today," says John Stott.[13]

The Laodicean church was self-satisfied. True satisfaction cannot be found in what this world offers; it can only be found in Christ. Chapter 8 mentioned that serving Jesus requires "go and die." Yet this is not about sacrifice, but satisfaction. I have met many people dissatisfied with life, and the common denominator was that they lived life for themselves or a cause. They were not living life with their eyes on Jesus and not finding satisfaction in Him. But a loving Savior is sure to try to bring people back to Him.

Loving Discipline

Jesus tells the church He corrects and disciplines those He loves. The best athlete receives the hardest training. Exceptional students have the most demanding tasks.[14]

Proverbs promotes reproof and discipline as expressions of love: "My child, don't reject the Lord's discipline, and don't be upset when he corrects you. For the Lord corrects those he loves, just as a father corrects a child in whom he delights" (Prov. 3:11-12 NLT).

Jesus knows us better than we know ourselves. He tells the Laodicean Christians, "I know your works…not realizing that you are…" (Rev. 3:15, 17). A person can deceive himself, but Jesus sees and knows everyone accurately. He instructs the church to turn from lukewarm ways to greater fervor for righteous living. Only in Jesus can that abundant life be found (John 10:10).

Reestablishing Fellowship

To the church in Laodicea, Jesus says, "Look! I stand at the door and knock" (Rev. 3:20). Jesus knocks at the entrance and wishes to enter and engage the occupant.

William Holman produced the famous painting *The Light of the World*, a scene of the risen Savior knocking on a door covered in overgrown weeds, long unopened. There was no handle on the outside. The door could only be opened from the inside. Establishing genuine fellowship with Jesus is a choice. He will not force entry.

In a blind self-sufficient manner the Laodicean church left Jesus outside. It acted like it could cope by itself. How easy to gain material things and at the same time bankrupt a soul.

Jesus requests permission to enter and establish fellowship. He desires to share a common meal, indicating a strong bond of affection and companionship. He does not wish to pass by but abide. Barclay explains, "It is not a mere courtesy visit, paid in the passing, which Jesus Christ offers to us. He desires to come in and to sit long with us, and to wait as long as we wish Him to wait."[15]

Jesus wants to be master of the house, no room remaining locked. Following Him means surrendering without condition, seeking His will and promptly obeying. Jesus instructed the disciples to pray, "Our Father in heaven, hallowed be your name. Your kingdom come, your will be done, on earth as it is in heaven" (Matt. 6:9-10). God's kingdom is where He rules and reigns. When people pray for God's kingdom to come, they ask Him to rule in their lives and situations, a dangerous yet exciting prayer. Have you brought yourself into submission with King Jesus?

The Promise

Not only does Jesus offer His presence in the lonely chambers of the heart, He offers His presence in the everyday battles of life, emerging unconquered and even conquering.[16]

Jesus sits on the throne in Revelation, a symbol of conquest and authority. To the victor, Jesus promises a shared throne. Paul promised, "If we endure hardship, we will reign with him" (2 Tim. 2:12). Christ was exalted to the Father's right hand, overcoming the world and the devil. Christian overcomers shall be honored as well.[17]

Mission Value: Fervently Abiding

Maintaining spiritual fervor involves abiding in Jesus, a principle given to the disciples shortly before the crucifixion. Jesus knew His departure was close and His disciples would no longer have opportunity to be with Him. They needed to learn to abide in a different way. Jesus instructed, "Abide in me, and I in you. As the branch cannot bear fruit by itself, unless it abides in the vine, neither can you, unless you abide in me. I am the vine; you are the branches. Whoever abides in me and I in him, he it is that bears much fruit, for apart from me you can do nothing" (John 15:4-5).

Abiding is a necessary prerequisite for fervor and fruitfulness. Maintaining fervor is dependent on receiving a constant flow of life from Christ. No spiritual achievement is possible while separate from Him. Apart from Him, a person can do nothing. Apart from Him, a person will not find meaning in life or hope for the future.

Apart from Him, a person can do nothing of lasting significance or anything of eternal value. Counter this with the words of Paul, "I can do all things through him who strengthens me" (Phil 4:13).

Abiding means "to remain," to stay in the presence of Jesus, to mediate on His Word, to constantly continue in prayer and worship, to remain in the mindset of Christ. As mentioned in Chapter 3, abiding includes reading the Bible, memorizing, praying, worshiping, and listening to the Spirit. Abiding increases knowledge of Him.

The book of Acts records an early Christian named Apollos visiting Ephesus who was "fervent in spirit" (Acts 18:25). He was well learned and motivated to tell others about Christ. Yet he still had things to learn. Priscilla and Aquila, early church planters, took him aside and explained the way of God more fully (v. 26).

The life of Apollos reveals that spiritual fervor involves engaging in mission. Abiding in Jesus gives strength to fulfill His mission. Abiding includes giving Jesus the best of our time, leading to the best of times.[18] Taking part in mission may not always seem like the best of times, but the spiritual growth and maturity gained is unparalleled. Mission involvement eventually leads to the best of times. It is important to take part in mission to be poured out for spiritual vitality.

Living in Jerusalem gives my family the opportunity to become familiar with the land of the Bible. Underground springs feed the Sea of Galilee, as does the Jordan River, which flows into the north side of the lake. At the south end, the Jordan River flows out to the Dead Sea. The waters of the Dead Sea flow nowhere. Everything stays there and nothing lives in the Dead Sea. Life requires a constant flow of nutrients—a filling up and a flowing out. Followers of Jesus need to be the Sea of Galilee, filled up by abiding and poured out in mission.

The quest for spiritual fervor and maturity is a lifelong endeavor. Paul says in Philippians 3:12-15,

> "Not that I have already obtained this or am already perfect, but I press on to make it my own, because Christ Jesus has made me his own. Brothers, I do not consider that I have made it my own. But one thing I do: forgetting what lies behind and straining forward to what lies ahead, I press on toward the goal for the prize of the upward call of God in Christ Jesus."

Even a veteran follower of Jesus like Paul did not view himself as having "arrived." There was more to learn and experience. He chose terms like "straining" and "pressing on" to describe a process. "The quest for spiritual maturity was not a passive or casual endeavor for Paul. He makes spiritual formation sound more like an athletic event than a Bible study."[19] Spiritual fervor requires abiding in perseverance and mission. To run the race well a person must remain aflame with a passion to change the world in Jesus' name.

The Message

A fervent passion for the things of God provides opportunity for a person to abide with Jesus on earth and reign with Him in heaven.

What things are keeping you hot for God? Are you attempting to follow Jesus while not doing His will? Have you lost the fervor of fresh faith? Have you put your trust in material things, leaving God out?

What a Great God

Jesus is presented as the "Amen." His ministry fulfills all the promises of God.[20] When people visit the church, do they say, "Wow, what a great church," or "Wow, what a great God"? A church with fervor points to Jesus and promises fulfillment in Him.

The War of the Lamb

Did the seven churches prove faithful? Did they refrain from participating in a culture of pagan religion and imperial worship, even when serious social, economic, and political consequences were involved? Were they willing to suffer like John, like Antipas of Pergamum (Rev. 2:13), and like Jesus?[21]

These churches were in a struggle, a war—the war of the Lamb. Believers will be victorious not by wielding swords but by following Jesus in worship and faithful witness.[22] Does the book of Revelation exalt martyrdom? The first-century meaning of "martyr" was "witness." Only later in church history did martyr refer to witnesses dying for their faith.[23] Revelation calls readers not to death, but to faithful discipleship and witness, even if leading to death. The message to the Church from the exalted Jesus is not a call to death but to discipleship, including abstaining from everything that defiles.[24] These messages reveal that faithful discipleship has costs and rewards. And the eternal reward far outweighs the temporary costs.

The Challenge

Nothing but a wholehearted commitment to Christ will do. Renew an earnest zeal, fervor, fire, and passion for God and His ways. "Seek the Kingdom of God above all else, and live righteously, and he will give you everything you need" (Matt. 6:33 NLT).

Small Group Discussion Starters

1. Follow-up from previous discussion: How did you engage in the mission of Jesus this week in your home, your neighborhood, your workplace and your church (proclamation, justice advocacy, peace-making, and acts of compassion)?

2. How could you provide refreshment for the spiritually weary and healing for the spiritually sick?
3. How does Jesus tell His followers they will experience "heaven on earth"?
4. In what ways have you found satisfaction in life?
5. In what areas of your life have you left Jesus on the outside?
6. Are you both abiding in Jesus and engaging in mission? If not, how can you start doing this today?

As a group hold each other accountable to abiding in Jesus and engaging in mission to maintain spiritual fervor. Pray and ask for God to revive the Church, beginning with you and your small group.

PART THREE

ENGAGING IN COMBAT

"I pray that when I die, all hell will have a party to celebrate the fact that I am no longer in the fight."

—C.T. Studd

Chapter Ten

CALLED TO CONFLICT

"There is no neutral ground in the universe. Every square inch, every split second, is claimed by God and counterclaimed by Satan."
–C. S. Lewis

To successfully engage in combat, a person must prepare for battle by keeping his or her eyes on Jesus through wilderness experiences and fully committing to a faith community—a place where he or she is genuinely known, lovingly supported, and honestly challenged. It is crucial to sharpen the steel by loving well, embracing suffering, walking in truth, exhibiting holiness, maintaining authentic faith, engaging in mission, and sustaining spiritual fervor. In this final section, engaging in combat, the church is called to conflict.

If God Be for Us

While serving as a high school administrator of an international school in a troubled East Jerusalem neighborhood, I was discussing some discipline matters one morning with Jeff, the dean of students. George, the director of operations, walked in seemingly out of breath. I gave him the token cultural greeting. He said Abu Ibrahim was on his way to talk about his son re-enrolling in school. Several weeks earlier, his son was expelled for repeated, abusive behavior as well as bullying.

Within a few minutes, Abu Ibrahim came down the hall escorted by our 6' 4", 330-pound school guard, Abdullah. The man appeared agitated, refused to sit down, and said he was upset that his son could not attend school. We discussed the situation. He calmed down and went on his way.

The next morning while helping George set up a businessmen's breakfast at the school, he told me God was watching out for me. "How?" I asked. It turns out Abu Ibrahim came into George's office irate and ready to hit me. He left George and headed toward my office. George headed my way but was stopped by someone along the way, so he told Abdullah to go to my office. George then quickly ran up two flights of stairs looking for Abu Ibrahim. The father had taken the elevator, but the electricity went out and he was trapped inside. By the time he arrived on my floor, Jeff and George were in my office, and Abdullah escorted him the rest of the way. He did not feel like hitting me with three big guys in the room.

Scripture tells us "we are not fighting against flesh-and-blood enemies, but against evil rulers and authorities of the unseen world, against mighty powers in this dark world, and against evil spirits in the heavenly places" (Eph. 6:12). We are not at war with those wanting to harm us, but with evil spirits and the evil one motivating people to make poor decisions. Our fight is not against people, government structures, or varying beliefs. Our battle is against the works of the devil.

A World at War

John writes, "The thief's purpose is to steal and kill and destroy" (John 10:10 NLT). My dad, a fellow minister, unpacks this verse to mean the mission of the evil accuser is to steal love for God, kill a desire for God, and destroy a witness for God. As stated earlier in the book, Peter declares, "Watch out for your great enemy, the devil. He prowls around like a roaring lion, looking for someone to devour" (1 Peter 5:8 NLT).

Why did Jesus come and die on a cross? Many would say, "Because my sin separates me from a holy God, and Jesus died that I might have a relationship with Him. His death reconciles me to God." In the first 1,000 years of church history, few people would have given that answer. They would have said, "To destroy the devil and his works."

Both are correct. The first response is individualistic. *My* sin separates *me* from God and Jesus came and died for *me* on the cross. The answer is focused on me. People who think this way find it hard to come together and share community with others. Community is where people are real with one another, encourage one another, and help one another. This kind of community is recorded in the book of Acts but rarely seen today.

John writes, "The reason the Son of God appeared was to destroy the works of the devil" (1 John 3:8). The mission of Jesus on earth is to defeat the enemy. The cross is victory over principalities and powers holding people in bondage—sin, death, and the devil. As emissaries believers are called and empowered to do the assignment established by the life, death, and resurrection of Jesus. He desires to build His church and advance His Kingdom through us. We live in a world at war, an ongoing battle between light and darkness, good versus evil. Jesus came to destroy the works of the devil and declared the gates of hell would not prevail against His advancing Kingdom.

The Church is called to conflict

Caesarea Philippi

Jesus first mentions the church in Matthew 16:13-19:

> Now when Jesus came into the district of Caesarea Philippi, he asked his disciples, "Who do people say that the Son of Man is?" And they said, "Some say John the Baptist, others say Elijah, and others Jeremiah or one of the prophets." He said to them, "But who do you say that I am?" Simon Peter replied, "You are the Christ, the Son of the living God." And Jesus answered him, "Blessed are you, Simon Bar-Jonah! For flesh and blood has not revealed this to you, but my Father who is in heaven. And I tell you, you are Peter, and on this rock I will build my church, and the gates of hell shall not prevail against it. I will give you the keys of the kingdom of heaven, and whatever you bind on earth shall be bound in heaven, and whatever you loose on earth shall be loosed in heaven."

Jesus travels with His disciples thirty miles north of Galilee to the district of Caesarea Philippi. In this region is an ancient Roman city at the southwestern base of Mount Hermon.

Nearby is a rocky hillside filled with shrines dedicated to false gods, the primary temple being to the god Pan. Next to the shrines is a large cave where a powerful stream once flowed. The temple to Pan stood over the entrance. The worshipers of Pan would perform human sacrifices in the cave and cast the remains into a natural abyss near the back.[1] The abyss was considered the entrance to Hades, a possible reference to the "gates of hell."[2] A victim disappearing in the water became a sign that the sacrifice was accepted. If blood appeared in the nearby springs, the sacrifice was considered rejected.

Cave at Caesarea Philippi

Removing the Veil

Jesus asked the disciples while visiting this region, "Who do people say that the Son of Man is?" The disciples knew the crowds saw Jesus as a prophet. People were veiled to the divine nature of Christ.

Shellie and I live where many women wear veils. In Sudan Shellie wore a headscarf everywhere we went. At first, it was part of a new adventure. Later, in 120-degree heat the veil became cumbersome. Shellie found ways to use it to her advantage. If we stopped at a light and a vehicle full of men stared at her, she took the scarf, put it in the visor, and created a veiled section in the truck.

Not only do physical veils on women exist in Sudan and East Jerusalem, but spiritual veils keep people throughout the world separated from God. Veils appear as materialism, busyness, pride, false religion—anything separating people from God. Jesus came to remove veils.

The disciples responded to Jesus, "Some say John the Baptist, others say Elijah, and others Jeremiah or one of the prophets." Jeremiah is an interesting choice. Why not Isaiah or one of the other major prophets? Jeremiah is known as a prophet of doom. He sustained opposition among his own people similar to Christ, and like Jesus predicted the destruction of the Temple.

Jesus asked the disciples, "But who do you say that I am?" The disciples witnessed many miracles and concluded He was the Son of God (Matt. 14:33). Peter replied, "You are the Christ, the Son of the living God." Peter formulated the growing recognition of the unique status and mission of Jesus. He recognized something was different about Him.

Shrines dedicated to false gods at Caesarea Philippi

Peter calls Jesus "the Son of the living God." The supernatural, dynamic Jesus came from the true God and was active in the world. The title marks Him as different from the false gods on the hillside. Peter recognizes he is standing in the presence of the living God while standing in the place where so-called gods were worshiped. Jesus commends Peter and reveals the divine source of this truth.

Paul writes, "But whenever someone turns to the Lord, the veil is taken away" (2 Cor. 3:16 NLT). A veil keeps people from recognizing Jesus. Believers tell others to see Jesus for who He is and then depend on the Holy Spirit to remove the veils of deception that prevent people from recognizing His divine nature. It is important to point people in the right direction.

What happens when a veil becomes lifted? "For the Lord is the Spirit, and wherever the Spirit of the Lord is, there is freedom. So all of us who have had that veil removed can see and reflect the glory of the Lord. And the Lord—who is the Spirit—makes us more and more like him as we are changed into his glorious image" (2 Cor. 3:17-18 NLT). Those once held captive experience freedom! They begin to reflect the glory of God and change into His glorious image. Christians need to turn people to Jesus and fulfill His command to advance God's Kingdom in the world.

A Firm Foundation

Jesus tells Peter that his declaration would be the foundation for advancing the Kingdom—"on this rock I will build my church" (Matt. 16:18). Jesus gives Peter a surname, like the renaming of Abram to Abraham, Sarai to Sarah, and Jacob to Israel. He refers to him as Petros representing the Aramaic "Kepha"—"stone" or "rock." Rocks provide a firm foundation for buildings. The Church would be built on Peter's proclamation, forever firm and secure. Joseph, the father of Jesus, was a builder, both a carpenter and mason. Stones are the primary building material in the land of Israel. Jesus will build His Church upon what rock?

Isaiah 51 sheds some light on the subject, "Listen to me, you who pursue righteousness, you who seek the Lord: look to the rock from which you were hewn, and to the quarry from which you were dug. Look to Abraham your father and to Sarah who bore you" (Isa. 51:1-2). A New Testament corollary reads, "You yourselves like living stones are being built up as a spiritual house" (1 Peter 2:5).

The church is built from the 4,000-year-old quarry of Abraham and Sarah, Isaac and Rebekah, Joseph, Deborah, David, Solomon, Isaiah, Mary and Joseph, Peter, John, Paul, and a great cloud of faithful witnesses. Paul declares,

> You are no longer strangers and aliens, but you are fellow citizens with the saints and members of the household of God, built on the foundation of the apostles and prophets, Christ Jesus himself being the cornerstone, in whom the whole structure, being joined together, grows into a holy temple in the Lord. In him you also are being built together into a dwelling place for God by the Spirit (Eph. 2:19-22).

The Church continues the mission of God, the redemption of God's creation. Jesus is the cornerstone upon which the New Testament Church is built with current members forming a structure to house the Spirit of God, a holy and awesome privilege and responsibility.

The Advancing Church

After speaking about building His church, Jesus refers to "the gates of hell," a metaphor for death and a striking contrast to the living God. In the place where false deities required human sacrifice, Jesus is the living God. God brings life, not death. Jesus promised, "I came that they may have life and have it abundantly" (John 10:10).

Genesis provides an account of Abraham willingly offering his son Isaac as a sacrifice. God intervenes and provides a ram. He tells Abraham,

> "Because you have done this and have not withheld your son, your only son, I will surely bless you, and I will surely multiply your offspring as the stars of heaven and as the sand that is on the seashore. And your offspring shall possess the gate of his enemies, and in your offspring shall all the nations of the earth be blessed, because you have obeyed my voice" (Gen. 22:16-18).

All nations are blessed by the coming of Jesus, the offspring of Abraham. His life, death, and resurrection provide a way for people to live in peace with God and each other.

Jesus' death on the cross provides the cornerstone for the divinely built Church. His resurrection, ascension, and sending of the Holy Spirit empowers the Church to the ends of the earth.

The Church wages war against lesser gods—destructive gods like Pan, Zeus, and the Imperial Cult. False gods focus on self, materialism, pride, fame, sex, and power, bringing death. The message of the Church is greater and the gates of hell, the gates of the enemy Satan, will not prevail against God's advancing Kingdom. The phrase "the gates of hell shall not prevail against it" does not suggest hiding in an impenetrable fortress. Jesus is not saying the devil is the aggressor and we are the defender. He is saying we are the aggressors and the devil is not safe from us. The Church charges on the offense, instead of hiding in foxholes, praying the shelling will stop.[3] We are an advancing Kingdom, assaulting the gates of hell.

How do we advance against the gates of hell? By charging them with love, justice, and peace! Advancement starts by taking every thought captive to Jesus and then valiantly pressing on:

> *Where there is despair, bring hope.*

Where there is unbelief, bring faith.
Where there is hatred, bring love.
Where there is bitterness, bring forgiveness.
Where there is sickness, offer healing.
Where there is disunity, offer reconciliation.

We are walking and talking representatives of Jesus to the world. John wrote, "For every child of God defeats this evil world, and we achieve this victory through our faith. And who can win this battle against the world? Only those who believe that Jesus is the Son of God" (1 John 5:4-5).

Whenever we turn people to Jesus, we storm the gates of hell. By digging water wells in Africa, we storm the gates of hell. By praying for the nations, we storm the gates of hell. When churches are established in areas where they do not exist, we storm the gates of hell. By displaying love and peace to the world, we advance the Kingdom of God. Jesus declares, "Look, I have given you authority over all the power of the enemy" (Luke 10:19 NLT). Walk in the authority of Christ and storm the gates of hell.

An Army of One

Ephesians instructs the Church in conflict to put on the whole armor of God and resist the enemy. The Church is an army engaged in battle, developing as a family. Conflict actually creates community, causing believers to depend on one another. Soldiers serving in the military become a band of brothers and sisters.

By entering conflict with others over the destiny of people and fighting toward the common goal of making disciples, community is formed. The Church forms genuine community by fighting alongside each other. The harder the fight, the more ingrained and tight-knit the community becomes. C. S. Lewis wrote, "Those who are going nowhere can have no fellow-travellers."[4] Others will not join someone heading nowhere. For those who desire community, engage in Kingdom-advancing work.

Paul encourages believers to stand firm in the faith, "Be on guard. Stand firm in the faith. Be courageous. Be strong" (1 Cor. 16:13 NLT). Peter encourages the same, "Resist [the devil], firm in your faith, knowing that the same kinds of suffering are being experienced by your brotherhood throughout the world" (1 Peter 5:9). Strength is found in numbers, not isolation. One cannot effectively advance the Kingdom of God on one's own. If someone tries to wage war on his own, the fight will be overwhelming. Stand shoulder to shoulder with other followers of Jesus and advance the Kingdom. Work with others toward a common goal. Together, the Church can make it happen.

> "Two people are better off than one, for they can help each other succeed. If one person falls, the other can reach out and help. But someone who falls alone is in real trouble… A person standing alone can be attacked and defeated, but two can stand back-to-back and conquer. Three are even better, for a triple-braided cord is not easily broken" (Ecc. 4:9-10,12 NLT).

When my wife and I brought our son Lucas home from the hospital, Shellie developed a stomach virus. Lucas began losing weight, causing elevated levels of bilirubin. Nate came home from school with a fever and runny nose. Haley was diagnosed with an upper respiratory infection. Not all sickness is an attack of the enemy, but there are times when he comes against you and the work of advancing the Kingdom of God. We recognized the attack and asked people within our faith community to come and pray for us. I sent emails to friends and family, asking them to pray. Within a day, Nate and Haley were healthy, Lucas gained weight, and Shellie's virus was gone.

We need one another. Paul refers to the Church as the Body of Christ, with everyone having an important function. You need the Church and the Church needs you.

Making Your Life Count

David Platt writes, "If you and I want our lives to count for God's purpose in the world, we need to begin with a commitment to God's people in the church. God has called us to lock arms with one another in single-minded, death defying obedience to one objective: the declaration of his gospel for the demonstration of his glory to all nations."[5] A commitment to God's people as the Church is required to advance the Kingdom. A commitment founded on love. Jesus declared, "There is no greater love than to lay down one's life for one's friends" (John 15:13).

In the *Lord of the Rings: Fellowship of the Ring*, a group of unlikely heroes make their way through a mountain. They encounter a massive being from the shadows and try to quickly work their way from the narrow passage. Gandalf, the grey wizard, turns to confront the evil beast with the declaration, "You shall not pass!" He stands in the gap for his comrades and the hideous creature eventually falls to the depths. As Gandalf turns towards his band of brothers, the beast takes one final shot with his fiery whip and hooks Gandalf's leg, causing him to trip, lose his grip, and fall into the pit.

Are we willing to fight like Gandalf? Fight with perseverance, love, truth, holiness, authenticity, and fervor? Fight for the souls of others? Fight on our knees in prayer? Enter into conflict for one another's well being.

Guarding the Flock

If we do not fight for one another, if we do not hold one another accountable for our actions, upholding love, truth, holiness, authenticity, mission, and fervor, we stand the risk of losing brothers and sisters. While talking with the disciples, Jesus stated,

> "If a man has a hundred sheep and one of them wanders away, what will he do? Won't he leave the ninety-nine others on the hills and go out to search for the one that is lost? And if he finds it, I tell you the truth, he will rejoice over it more than over the ninety-nine that didn't wander away! In the same way, it is not my heavenly Father's will that even one of these little ones should perish" (Matt. 18:12-14).

Is He talking about Christians who wander away from the truth? Biblically functioning communities go after wandering sheep and save them from the enemy. If only one member of a church is in spiritual danger, action must be taken to bring him or her back, to restore that person in the battalion once again. Everyone matters and working together is of primary importance.

Promised Victory

When we work together, what does Jesus say will happen? *"They shall not prevail against us!"* Victory has been promised. We simply need to willingly advance on the gates of our evil enemy. Are you willing? The battle may be difficult but God is on our side. The keys of the Kingdom have been given to the Church.

The Conquering Church

Asia Minor, the location of the seven churches of Revelation, was united in material luxury by Roman roads but utterly confused in religious matters. In Ephesus the great mother of gods Artemis reigned. Alongside her were lesser Greek and Roman gods and growing Imperial worship. Every city contained temples for various gods and religions.

The seven letters to the churches concluded with "to the one who conquers." The Christian church is a conquering force. The worship of Artemis (Diana) lasted 1,400 years, yet the strength of the message of Jesus destroyed this within a few years of strategic Spirit-led mission. The book of Acts records within two years all the residents of Asia heard the message of Jesus (Acts 19:10). By the second century, Pliny the Younger started investigating Christianity and found so many that he became worried.[6]

"Great Pan is dead," Plutarch once wrote, describing the lament of passengers sailing along the west coast of Greece. The god of shepherds and flocks had died and the Christian faith had triumphed over paganism.[7]

When Constantine the Great adopted Christianity as the state religion, the pagan temples received a mortal blow. The images of Artemis were defaced, her statues destroyed or buried, and her name erased from inscriptions. Pagan wall paintings were plastered over or scraped off. Statues were sent to kilns or crosses were carved on their foreheads. Churches were erected from the material of Roman monuments and pagan temples.[8]

James Kennedy, founder of Evangelism Explosion, made this observation: When Peter preached his first sermon, over 3,000 believed. Shortly thereafter 5,000 were added, followed by a great multitude of Jews and priests. Next came a period of persecution. When it ended in AD 313 with the Edict of Toleration, ten million professing Christians were alive. By the year 1,000, the number had grown to fifty million. By the end of the 1700's there were 215 million professing Christians, an increase of 169 million in eight hundred years. By 1900 the number had grown to 500 million. By 1990, the number was roughly 1.8 billion, an increase of 1.3 billion people in the 20th century alone.[9]

David Barrett, a church demographer, compared the estimated number of committed believers with the number of non-believing people in the world at different points in time.

- By 1430, 1 out of 99 followed Jesus.
- By 1790, 1 out of 49.
- By 1960, 1 out of 24.
- By 1980, 1 out of 16.

- By 1993, 1 out of 9 followed Jesus.[10]

The Church is fulfilling its mission to make disciples. Every believer must tell the story of Jesus until all have heard!

Not a Military Battle

The Church is a conquering force but not militaristic. Early Christians were never fascinated with the power of the Roman military. They clung to the cross where evil is conquered, not by swords and spears but by suffering and love. Jesus said to love Him by obeying His commands, including loving your enemies, not killing them.

Evil is fought not by military might but with the message of Jesus, enduring persecution for a mightier plan. Jesus in the Garden of Gethsemane renounced the sword and turned away from the use of force.[11] His peaceful method eventually conquered Rome and other barbarian kingdoms. The famous Roman sword and fearsome barbarian axes and clubs were all laid at the feet of the Prince of Peace.[12]

The Church's weapons of warfare are love, truth, holiness, authentic faith, and fervor. We defeat evil by rewarding those influenced by it (Matt. 5:40-41). We bless those who persecute us (Rom. 12:14). We turn the other cheek when slapped with insults (Matt. 5:39). The world is changed through sacrifice, dying to self, and giving of self to others in imitation of Jesus' great sacrifice. This is how the Church fights evil in the world. We overcome evil with good (Rom. 12:21).

Engaged in Conflict

"Mary Slessor was a fire-filled Scottish redhead accustomed to fighting thugs in Dundee with her fists. She went to Africa and fought slave traders and baby killers, giving her life to the Calabar people and fighting for the rights of African women. She lived for forty years in a mud hut, and thousands of Africans mourned her when she died in 1915. Her African name was 'Mother of All Peoples.' Mary cultivated a lifelong habit of chatting with her heavenly Father out loud and incessantly. It was Slessor who coined the phrase 'God plus one are always a majority.'"[13]

Keeping Your Eyes on Jesus

Engaging in battle can cause weariness. If believers take their eyes off Jesus, perseverance becomes difficult. John, on the island of Patmos, persevered by living in the Spirit. To battle well Christians must abide well. An ability to endure hardship requires time spent with Jesus.

Abiding is part of the battle plan. Dick Brodgen unpacks John 15 in *Live Dead: The Journey*. He writes, "The fruit of abiding is the harvest of people."[14] While abiding in Him, ask the Holy Spirit to unveil Jesus (John 15:7), gather in a harvest of lost people (v. 5), and provide opportunity to participate in the greater works of Jesus (14:12).

Jesus ascended to heaven and sent the Holy Spirit to dwell within those calling Him Lord (John 16:7). Our role is to be filled with the Spirit, abide in Jesus, advance His Kingdom worldwide, and defeat the schemes of the devil. His will is for none to perish (2 Peter 3:9).

Build Your Kingdom Here

The song "Build Your Kingdom Here" should be the anthem of the Church:

Come set Your rule and reign
In our hearts again
Increase in us we pray
Unveil why we're made

Come set our hearts ablaze with hope
Like wildfire in our very souls
Holy Spirit come invade us now
We are Your Church
We need Your power
In us

We seek Your Kingdom first
We hunger and we thirst
Refuse to waste our lives
For You're our joy and prize
To see the captive hearts released
The hurt; the sick; the poor at peace
We lay down our lives for Heaven's cause
We are Your church
We pray revive
This Earth

Build Your Kingdom here
Let the darkness fear
Show Your mighty hand
Heal our streets and land
Set Your Church on fire
Win this nation back
Change the atmosphere
Build Your Kingdom here
We pray

Unleash Your Kingdom's power
Reaching the near and far
No force of hell can stop
Your beauty changing hearts
You made us for much more than this
Awake the Kingdom seed in us
Fill us with the strength and love of Christ

We are Your church
We are the hope
On earth[15]

Mission Value: Fighting a Battle

Dietrich Bonhoeffer clarifies the commission,

> Jesus Christ lived in the midst of his enemies. In the end all his disciples abandoned him. On the cross he was all alone, surrounded by criminals and the jeering crowds. He had come for the express purpose of bringing peace to the enemies of God. So Christians, too, belong not in the seclusion of a cloistered life but in the midst of enemies. There they find their mission, their work. "To rule is to be in the midst of your enemies. And whoever will not suffer this does not want to be part of the rule of Christ; such a person wants to be friends and sit among the roses and lilies, not with the bad people but the religious people. O you blasphemers and betrayers of Christ! If Christ had done what you are doing, who would ever have been saved?" (Luther).[16]

While teaching in the Chicago area, Shellie and I volunteered as young couple ministers at the Stone Church. A small group of young couples in the church grew to several couples regularly meeting for Bible study, spiritual formation, and life-on-life ministry. Shellie and I prayed for and encouraged other couples to join.

During Shellie's first year teaching in Tinley Park, she mentored another elementary teacher, a fun-loving family man who enjoyed running. I occasionally interacted with him. At some school functions he wore comical clothes while interacting with students. He and his wife did not attend the small group, but we stayed in contact after moving to Sudan and later to Jerusalem.

Their family and ours are blessed with three children, both having two boys and a girl.

Shellie received an email in Jerusalem from a teacher about her former colleague. He was hit by a commuter train and died. We were devastated. Within days, a report came that it was not an accident. He took his own life. We grieved for him, his wife, and three children, as well as the school and community. We regretted not making a greater effort to address his eternal well-being and not doing more to get them involved with our group.

We are in a battle. As C. S. Lewis stated, "There is no neutral ground." Be willing to fight for the souls of others. Family members and work colleagues may be a moment away from eternal separation from God. Will we speak truth in love? Will we display authentic faith to those around us? If necessary, are we willing to suffer for the cause of Christ so others can experience eternity with God? Will we walk through doors of opportunity? Will we fulfill the command of Jesus to go into the world and make disciples?

Called to Conflict

We are called and must fight for community. We are called and must fight for love. We are called and must fight with purpose. Fight for your faith and the faith of your neighbor. Enter into conflict for truth, holiness, authenticity, and fervor.

The Message

Jesus sent letters to seven churches revealing He died for the Church, is in the midst of her, loves her, and gave her an assignment. The hope of the world is Jesus, the message of the Church.

The Challenge

The coming of Jesus and the building of His church dealt a mortal blow to pagan religions. Matthew records, "And this gospel of the kingdom will be proclaimed throughout the whole world as a testimony to all nations, and then the end will come" (Matt. 24:14). Will the global Church remain committed to the mission of God on the earth and drive the demonic invaders out?

Jesus initiated a revolution. All He wants is a few who will think as He did, love as He did, see as He did, and serve as He did. All He needs is to revolutionize the hearts of a few, and they will impact the world.[17]

Presently over three billion people are without the message of Jesus. Will you join the resistance? Will you commit yourself to Christ and the Church and storm the gates of hell until His imminent return? You are the Church, the hope of the world!

Small Group Discussion Starters

1. <u>Follow-up from previous discussion:</u> In what areas of your life did you allow Jesus full entrance? How did you abide and engage in mission to grow your spiritual fervor?
2. What are some practical ways you could bring others to Jesus, making it possible for the Holy Spirit to remove the numerous veils of unbelief?
3. Who are you standing in the gap for? List the names of five people that God wants you to spiritually contend for.
4. How can you fight for community? For love? For truth? For holiness? For authenticity? For fervor?
5. What are some ways you, your small group, or your church can begin storming the gates of hell in your family? In your neighborhood? In your workplace? In your city? In your nation? In the world?
6. What is limiting your courage to storm the gates of hell?

As a group hold each other accountable to do what the Holy Spirit lays on your heart. Pray for God to give you the ability to hear what the Spirit is saying and for feet quick to obey.

The Eleventh Chapter

CALLED TO LISTEN

"A letter to the church in…"

All seven letters conclude, "Anyone with ears to hear must listen to the Spirit and understand what he is saying."[1] A critical component of Revelation 2 and 3 includes listening to the Spirit of God as He identifies the local church's current state, then asking Jesus to transform her into a more faithful community.[2]

A hearing ear is one in which there is faith and obedience. The Spirit speaks in various ways. One way is through the Bible, the inspired Word of God (2 Peter 1:21). A spiritual mentor, Dr. Mike Rakes, says the Spirit speaks through "God thoughts" (Acts 10:19, 11:12, 13:2). And the Spirit speaks through the grace gifts recorded in 1 Corinthians 12, both privately and in community (Acts 2:4; 1

Cor. 12:4–10, 28). Pray and ask for the Holy Spirit to speak, having ears to hear what He says.

We stop living abundantly for Christ when we no longer listen to the Spirit. If we want to keep walking in truth, we must keep our ears open to the Spirit of God. And the Holy Spirit speaks to those living a holy life.

Hearing is directly linked to overcoming. In each of the letters to the churches, the hearer is one who listens, responds, and conquers. A conquering church must first be a listening and responsive community.

Readers, small groups, and congregations are encouraged to take time collectively to listen to the Spirit and compose a personal letter for their faith community. Make the letter similar to what is found in the book of Revelation.

Pray and ask:

5. How would Jesus describe himself? He listed unique qualities to every church He addressed in Revelation. This may be better answered after working through the next three questions.
6. What commendation would Jesus give? What good things are happening within your church? Remember, the church is called to perseverance, community, love, suffering, truth, holiness, authenticity, mission, fervor, and conflict.
7. What points of correction would Jesus address? What things should the church turn from or begin doing?
8. What promise can the church expect by fulfilling what Christ asks of them?

Chapter 2 ("Called to Community") mentions God is best revealed through a body of believers. Put together a letter that collectively represents and speaks to your faith community.

We did this exercise with our church in Jerusalem. We asked everyone to take time to pray, read the Word, spend time singing to the Lord and, most of all, listen to the Spirit. People emailed answers to the questions listed above and a church elder compiled the responses into a unified letter to the church. He pulled heavily from Scripture, wanting the faith community to speak through the Word to our church. You can find a copy of the letter in Appendix 1.

The church then came together, read the letter, celebrated the things going well, and talked through practical solutions to the points of correction. It was a great exercise for the church and helped us grow in community. We deepened our love for one another.

The Challenge

The letter writing is an exercise in vulnerability and trust. Is your church open to the Spirit speaking and potentially putting a finger on sore spots? Will it make changes to better represent Jesus to the world?

When your church has finished creating a Spirit-sensitive letter, email a copy to letters@theresistancemovement.com. The letter will be posted online to reference how the Spirit is speaking to the Church today.

Appendix 2 lists recommended reading in response to the letter for your church. Each book listed corresponds with the characteristics found in that chapter. I encourage you, your small group, and your church to continue to grow into Christ's vision for the Church.

Conclusion

JOIN THE MOVEMENT

"Some wish to live within the sound of chapel bells.
I wish to run a rescue mission within a yard of hell."
–C. T. Studd

When Jesus invited the first disciples to "follow me," they probably didn't imagine they would become part of a movement that would change the world. Within a few years, they were accused of turning the world upside down (Acts 17:6) and within a couple hundred years, "Pan was dead" and the Imperial Cult toppled. Jesus is building His Church, and we have an invitation to participate.

What does it mean to join the Resistance? It means to make a commitment to King Jesus and the people in His Church.

1. *A person must first be willing to recognize his or her need for help.* Paul writing to the Christians in Rome explains, "For everyone has sinned; we all fall short of God's glorious standard" (Rom. 3:23 NLT).
2. *A person needs to understand Jesus came and died for his or her sins and to destroy the works of the devil.* Paul continues, "God showed his great love for us by sending Christ to die for us while we were still sinners" (Rom. 5:8 NLT). And John explains, "The reason the Son of God appeared was to destroy the works of the devil" (1 John 3:8).
3. *An individual must respond to Jesus' request to "follow me," making Him the center of his or her life.* Paul writes, "If you confess with your mouth that Jesus is Lord and believe in your heart that God raised him from the dead, you will be saved. For it is by believing in your heart that you are made right with God, and it is by confessing with your mouth that you are saved…For 'Everyone who calls on the name of the Lord will be saved'" (Rom. 10:9–10, 13 NLT).
4. *A person needs to make a commitment to a local body of believers, being genuinely known, lovingly supported, and honestly challenged.*

Once a person has made Jesus and His Church a priority, a decision to live according to "Resistance" values is important. The members of our church in Jerusalem are challenged to live up to three expectations:[1]

1. Love Jesus and others (John 14:15; Mark 12:30–31; Matt. 28:19–20).
2. Live in the joy of the Lord (James 1:2–4).
3. Run the race well (2 Tim. 4:7-8; Heb. 12:1–2).

You know you are living by these standards by evaluating how much time you spend with Jesus and others. If you love Him, you will abide in Him. If you love others, you spend time serving them. A person can gauge how joyful he or she is by how often he or she avoids complaining and whining over life circumstances. A joyful person does not whine. Finally, an individual can measure how well he or she runs the race by not quitting. Remain engaged in the world and maintain effectiveness in God's Kingdom.

The Challenge

Commit to Jesus and the Church. Decide to abide with a "Resistance" mindset by loving God and others, living in the joy of the Lord, and running the race well. Go online today (theresistancemovement.com) and sign up to be a part of the movement. Change the world!

APPENDICES

Appendix 1

A LETTER TO THE CHURCH IN JERUSALEM

"Write this letter to the angel of New Life Church in Jerusalem. This is the message from the One who sits on the heavenly throne, the Lover of all people, who called you and equipped you for every good work (Eph. 2:10). The Champion who initiates and perfects your faith. (Heb. 12:2)

I know all the things you do. I have seen your sacrifices, your hard work and your patient endurance (Rev. 2:2). I have opened a door for you that no one can close (3:8). I see your good intentions and your desire to make my Name famous. Persevere patiently, for my Name will be made great throughout the land. Relate what you have seen as inspiration for others.

I have asked you to die daily and follow me (1 Cor. 15:31; Matt. 16:24). Do not be afraid to share in My sufferings (Phil. 3:10).

As you obey my command to share each other's burdens (Gal. 6:2) and persevere, I will give you character displayed by the fruit of the Spirit; love, joy, peace, patience, kindness, goodness, faithfulness, gentleness, and self-control (Rev. 3:10; Rom. 5:3–4; Gal. 5:22–23).

Do not let anyone think less of you because you are young. Be an example to all believers in what you say, in the way you live, in your love, your faith, and your purity (1 Tim. 4:12). Live a life above reproach (1 Tim. 3:2).

But I have this complaint against you. You don't love Me or each other as deeply as you should. Be careful that your previous sacrifices of home and comfort do not give you an excuse to be complacent. Keep your eyes on Me by abiding in Me for I have more to ask of you. In unity, devote yourselves to prayer; the study, teaching and proclaiming of My Word (Acts 6:4; Col. 4:2; 1 Tim. 2:1; 2 Tim. 2:15; Matt. 28:19–20). Maintain authentic relationships with one another by lovingly speaking truth and being accountable to one another.

I am coming soon. All who are victorious will be citizens in the city of my God—the new Jerusalem that comes down from heaven from my God (Rev. 3:11–12), a place of peaceful rest.

Anyone with ears to hear must listen to the Spirit and understand what He is saying to the churches."

Appendix 2

RECOMMENDED READING

The Church

Center Church - Timothy Keller

Chapter 1: Called to the Wilderness

A Pathway Through Suffering - Elisabeth Elliot

Chapter 2: Called to Community

Sticky Church - Larry Osborne

Chapter 3: Called to Love

The Four Loves - C.S. Lewis

Chapter 4: Called to Suffer

The Insanity of God - Nik Ripken

Chapter 5: Called to Truth

Multiply - Francis Chan

Chapter 6: Called to Holiness

The Challenge of the Disciplined Life - Richard Foster

Chapter 7: Called to Authenticity

Dying Out Loud - Shawn Smucker

Chapter 8: Called to Mission

Introducing the Missional Church - Alan J. Roxburgh & M. Scott Boren

Chapter 9: Called to Fervor

The Pursuit of God - A. W. Tozer

Chapter 10: Called to Conflict

Radical Together - David Platt

Appendix 3

MAKING DISCIPLES

"God has entrusted us with his most precious treasure—people. He asks us to shepherd and mold them into strong disciples, with brave faith and good character."
–John Ortberg

Before ascending into heaven, Jesus gave instruction to His disciples: "Therefore, go and make disciples of all the nations, baptizing them in the name of the Father and the Son and the Holy Spirit. Teach these new disciples to obey all the commands I have given you. And be sure of this: I am with you always, even to the end of the age" (Matt. 28:19-20 NLT).

Jesus commands His followers to make disciples who form churches. Someone could ask what makes a person a disciple? Or how do we define church? If we are asked by King Jesus to make disciples, it is important to know what we are aiming for. Thanks to Dick, Rob, Caleb, Brent, and others who contributed to the definitions below.

Disciple

A disciple is someone who has received the Spirit by believing the gospel and by putting his/her faith in Jesus as Lord.

Marks of a Maturing Disciple

A maturing disciple should be in community (a church) growing in his/her faith, obedience, and understanding of Jesus. A maturing disciple is formed into God's image as he/she walks with, studies, and imitates Christ. A maturing disciple is someone who is led by the Spirit (Rom. 8:14), grows in gospel understanding and practice (2 Pet. 3:18), and increasingly obeys the Lord Jesus (John 15:14). A maturing disciple is baptized with water (Acts 1:5), filled with the Holy Spirit for empowered witness (Acts 1:8), abides in Jesus and His Word (John 15:5–7), makes disciples (Matt. 28:19), is mission-hearted (Acts 15:19), grows in doctrine, fellowship, communion (sacrament), and prayer, (Acts 2:42), is generous and sacrificial (Matt. 5:42; Acts 2:44), demonstrates the fruit of the Spirit (Gal. 5:22-23), and follows the way of the cross (John 12:24; Gal. 2:20).

Definition of an Emerging Local Church Theologically

Disciples joined together by the Holy Spirit in tangible fellowship.

Description of an Emerging Local Church in Terms of Practice

Baptized disciples (Acts 2:38) joined together by the Holy Spirit who regularly meet together for the study of God's Word, fellowship, communion, and prayer (Acts 2:42).

Marks of a Maturing Church

A healthy church is a local expression of God's eschatological, new covenant community of repentant disciples born of the Spirit, saved from sin and death, and reconciled to the Father and to one another through the gospel of Jesus the Son. This community lives by the Spirit in unity, holiness, global relationship, and accountability to Scripture. Filled with the Spirit and walking in the miraculous, the church is shaped in God's image, empowered to live for His honor, and centered on worship that leads to mission to all peoples. The church follows the way of the cross and in suffering participates in the extension of God's reign in the world, inviting all to restored relationship with God in the gospel; the church is both recipient and conduit of God's love. In expression of its life and mission, the church multiplies, spawning new communities of faith both near and far.

Jesus build Your Church as Your followers live out Your Word as a community who enjoys the goodwill of all people, while making disciples, and the Lord adding daily to the number who believe (Acts 2:47). May the global church be strengthened in faith and growing larger everyday (16:5)!

ACKNOWLEDGEMENTS

This book started as a conversation with a work colleague about the centrality of Jesus in the life of every Christian. It then catalyzed during a family trip to Turkey where I became intrigued with the early church. The question "What does Jesus expect of His Church?" drove the content. I am indebted to:

Johnny and Murad, for letting me use their jewelry piece as a symbol for this book.

Francis, for transferring the jewelry piece to a digital wax seal.

The talented crew at Prodigy Pixel, for their graphic work on the cover.

Joe, for putting together the book trailer and video for Chapter 10.

Boshra and Ann, for letting me share your family stories.

Pat, for allowing me to transmit some of your understanding related to the Spirit's work in a believer's life.

Taylor, for the idea for the eleventh chapter.

Aaron, Nick, and Nikole, for your willingness to review initial drafts to generate clear content.

Mark, Bernhard, Erene, Shane, and others, for praying that this book serves as a catalyst for growth of mission in the Church.

Jackie, Sarah, Stephen and others for polishing the final product so others might be willing to read it.

Ross, for teaching me so much more about Jesus.

My dad, for our conversations regarding the book's content, your willingness to edit every word, and your example to love Jesus and His Church.

Nate, Haley, and Lucas, my three exuberant kids. I'm proud to be your dad and delighted to see Jesus in each of you.

Shellie, my beloved wife and partner, whose encouragement and support have been an inspiration from beginning to end. It is a joy serving King Jesus with you by my side.

The faith community at New Life Church Jerusalem. It is a joy to serve you for God's glory in the Holy Land.

My co-laborers around the world who work to drive the invader from their territory everyday. Thank you for faithfully serving in The Resistance.

ABOUT THE AUTHOR

Zach is a cross-cultural minister, educator, speaker, and writer. He oversaw international schools in both Khartoum, Sudan, and Jerusalem, Israel, and currently serves as lead pastor of New Life Church in Jerusalem.

Zach and his family lived in Khartoum for two years and now reside in East Jerusalem. Through their work, Zach and his family encourage others to live according to the teachings of Jesus and promote positive change in their communities and nations. Zach and Shellie, along with their three children, long to see Jesus unveiled in the hearts and minds of people around the world.

Zach maintains a blog at zachmaddox.com, produces podcasts on iTunes, publishes video Bible teachings at vimeo.com/zachmaddox, and posts daily inspiration on Twitter: @zachmaddox.

NOTES

How to Use This Book

[1] C.S. Lewis, *The Four Loves,* (New York, NY: First Mariner Books, 2012), 89.

Introduction

[1] Os Guinness, *Renaissance*, (Downers Grove, IL: InterVarsity Press, 2014), 137.

Chapter One: Called to the Wilderness

[1] Carl Medearis, *Speaking of Jesus: The Art of Non-Evangelism*, (Colorado Springs, CO: David C Cook, 2011), 54.
[2] Francis Chan, *Crazy Love*, (Colorado Springs, CO: David C Cook, 2008), 17.
[3] Oswald Chambers, *My Utmost for His Highest*, (Grand Rapids, MI: Discovery House Publishers, 1992), April 9.
[4] A. W. Tozer, *The Pursuit of God*, (Harrisburg, PA: Christian Publications, Inc., 1948), 11.
[5] I borrowed this term with permission from Mark Renfroe, a friend and colleague who understands well what it means to be gloriously deconstructed.
[6] Alicia Britt Chole, *Anonymous*, (Nashville, TN: Integrity Publishers, 2006), 50.

Chapter Two: Called to Community

[1] Chuck Miller, *The Spiritual Formation of Leaders*, (Xulon Press, 2007), 172.
[2] Andy Stanley, *Deep & Wide*, (Grand Rapids, MI: Zondervan, 2012), 49.
[3] Ibid, 52.
[4] Miller, 173–174.
[5] Ibid, 178.
[6] Dietrich Bonhoeffer, *Life Together and Prayerbook of the Bible*, (Minneapolis, MN: Fortress Press, 2005), 105.
[7] Larry Osborne, Sermon, James River Church, Springfield, MO, September 8, 2014.
[8] Julie Gorman, *Community That Is Christian: A Handbook on Small Groups*, (Wheaton, IL: Victor Books, 1993), 16–17.
[9] Guinness, 28.

---

[10] Steve Smith, *T4T: A Discipleship Re-Revolution*, (Monument, CO: WIGTake Resources, 2011), Chapter 4, Obedience-based versus Knowledge-based Maturity, para. 1.
[11] Ibid, Chapter 4, The Two Sons, para. 2.
[12] Ibid, Chapter 4, The Scribe in the Kingdom, para. 2.
[13] Stanley, 53.

Chapter Three: Called to Love

[1] John Stott, *What Christ Thinks of the Church*, (Grand Rapids, MI: Baker Books, 2003), 10.
[2] Mark Wilson, *Biblical Turkey: A Guide to the Jewish and Christian Sites of Asia Minor*, (Istanbul: Yayinlari, 2012), 201.
[3] William Barclay, *Letters to the Seven Churches*, (Louisville, KY: Westminster John Know Press, 2001), 6.
[4] Wilson, 202.
[5] Stott, 29.
[6] Ibid, 28.
[7] A.W. Tozer, *The Pursuit of God*, (Harrisburg, PA: Christian Publications, Inc., 1948), 75.
[8] Timothy Keller, *Center Church*, (Grand Rapids, MI: Zondervan, 2012), Chapter 13, para. 1.
[9] Everett Ferguson, *Backgrounds of Early Christianity*, (Grand Rapids, MI: Eerdmans Publishing Co., 2003), Chapter 6, Attitudes of Pagans Toward Christians, para. 3.
[10] Keller, Chapter 12, City Ministry in the Early Church, para. 2.
[11] Ibid, Chapter 13, para. 2.
[12] Ibid, Chapter 13, para 2 & 3.
[13] Ibid, Chapter 13, Globalization and Renaissance, para. 2.
[14] Ibid, Chapter 13, The Challenge of Ministry in Cities, para. 6.
[15] Ibid, Chapter 11, The City of Exile, para. 2.
[16] Ibid, Chapter 11, para. 2.
[17] Ibid, Chapter 11, Israel and the City, para. 2.
[18] Ibid, Chapter 11, The Prophets and the City, para. 1.
[19] Ibid, Chapter 11, The Prophets and the City, para. 1.
[20] Ibid, Chapter 12, para. 3.
[21] Ibid, Chapter 12, Consummation: Cultivating the City, para. 1.
[22] Ibid, Chapter 13, The Opportunity of Ministry in Cities, para. 12.

Chapter Four: Called to Suffer

[1] Nik Ripken, *The Insanity of God*, (Nashville, TN: B&H Publishing Group, 2013), 231.
[2] Wilson, 309.

[3] Ibid.
[4] Barclay, 16.
[5] Ferguson, Chapter 6, Attitudes of Pagans Toward Christians, para. 8.
[6] Barclay, 19.
[7] Wilson, 280.
[8] Ferguson, Chapter 6, The Legal Status of Christianity, para. 1.
[9] Wilson, 309.
[10] Wilson, 309.
[11] Stott, 38.
[12] S. Robert Maddox, *Action: Reflections from the Gospel of Mark*, (Redefining Faith Resources, 2013), 7.
[13] Stott, 42.
[14] Ibid, 43.
[15] James C. Denison, "Respected to Irrelevant to Dangerous: Does Religion Poison Everything," (Dallas, TX: Denison Forum, Aug. 2014), 4.
[16] Ibid.
[17] Ripken, 231.
[18] Stott, 47.
[19] Walter J. Ciszek, *He Leadeth Me*, (New York, NY: Doubleday, 1975), 84-89.
[20] David Platt, *Radical*, (Colorado Springs, CO: Multnomah Books, 2010), 56.
[21] Elisabeth Elliot, *A Path Through Suffering*, (Ventura, CA: Regal, 1990), 197-199.
[22] Credited to G.K. Chesterton
[23] Elliot, 89.
[24] Barclay, 23.
[25] Ibid, 26.
[26] Stanley, 50.
[27] Ripken, 153.
[28] Joaquin Miller. Columbus. 1892.
[29] Ibid, Foreword, para. 3.
[30] Barclay, 28.
[31] Stott, 48.
[32] Ripken, 308.

Chapter Five: Called to Truth

[1] Wilson, 290.
[2] Kenneth Bailey. *Jesus Through Middle Eastern Eyes*. (Downers Grove, IL: InterVarsity Press, 2008), Chapter 21, para. 1.
[3] Wilson, 284.
[4] Platt, 37.

---

[5] Francis Frangipane, *The Three Battlegrounds,* (Cedar Rapids, IA: Arrow Publications, 2006), 63.
[6] Barclay, 35.
[7] Barclay, 36.
[8] Ferguson, Chapter 6, Hindrances to the Acceptance of Christianity, para. 1.
[9] Barclay, 40.
[10] Stott, 51.
[11] Ibid, 57.
[12] Ibid, 57.
[13] Ibid, 51-52.
[14] Chambers, June 26th.
[15] Os Guinness. *Prophetic Untimeliness.* (Grand Rapids, MI: Baker Books, 2003), 89.
[16] Ibid, 106.
[17] Ibid, 100.
[18] Stott, 62.
[19] Barclay, 42.
[20] Francis Chan, *Multiply,* (Colorado Springs, CO: David C. Cook, 2012), 16.
[21] Dietrich Bonhoeffer, *The Cost of Discipleship,* (New York, NY: Touchstone, 1995), 59.
[22] Chan, 16, 20.
[23] Chambers, July 2nd.
[24] Chan, 14.
[25] Platt, 7.

Chapter Six: Called to Holiness

[1] Richard Foster, *The Challenge of the Disciplined Life: Christian Reflections on Money, Sex & Power,* (San Francisco, CA: Harper Collins, 1985), 1.
[2] Wilson, 319.
[3] Barclay, 45.
[4] Barclay, 50.
[5] Stott, 66.
[6] Barclay, 50.
[7] Ibid, 47.
[8] Elliot, 79.
[9] Barclay, 48.
[10] Wilson, 320.
[11] Christopher J. H. Wright, *The Mission of God's People: A Biblical Theology of the Church's Mission,* (Grand Rapids, MI: Zondervan, 2010), Chapter 1, What Kind of People Are We?, para. 3.

[12] Stott, 69.
[13] DC Talk. "What If I Stumble." From *Jesus Freak*. (Forefront Records. 1995.)
[14] Stanley, 206.
[15] Stott, 73.
[16] Barclay, 53.
[17] Barclay, 54.
[18] Ibid, 55.
[19] Wilson, 319.
[20] David Platt, *Follow Me,* (Carol Stream, IL: Tyndale, 2013), 85.

Chapter Seven: Called to Authenticity

[1] Shawn Smucker, *Dying Out Loud,* (Springfield, MO: Influence Resources, 2013), Chapter 4, para. 19.
[2] Wilson, 296.
[3] Ibid, 304.
[4] Barclay, 57.
[5] Ibid.
[6] Barclay, 64.
[7] Stott, 85.
[8] Guinness, *Renaissance*, 114.
[9] Barclay, 65.
[10] Stott, 90.
[11] Ibid, 92.
[12] Stott, 93.
[13] Wilson, 308.
[14] Keller, Chapter 9, Paul's Speeches in Acts, para. 5.
[15] Ibid, Chapter 9, para. 1.
[16] Ibid, Chapter 9, Romans 1-2 and the Mixed Nature of Culture, para. 1.
[17] Ibid, Chapter 9, Romans 1-2 and the Mixed Nature of Culture, para. 7.
[18] Ibid, Chapter 9, First Corinthians 1 and the Biblical Balance, para. 5.
[19] Platt, *Radical,* 35-36.
[20] Ibid, 36.
[21] Keller, Chapter 10, para. 6; Entering and Adapting to the Culture, para. 1.
[22] Ibid, Chapter 10, Appealing to and Consoling the Listeners, para. 2.
[23] Ibid, Chapter 10, Appealing to and Consoling the Listeners, para. 4.
[24] Stott, 95.
[25] Smucker, Chapter 6, para. 14.

Chapter Eight: Called to Mission

[1] Hudson Taylor (1832-1905).

---

[2] Barclay, 67.
[3] Stanley, 231.
[4] Ibid, 240.
[5] Ibid, 255.
[6] Ibid, 256.
[7] Dick Brogden, *Live Dead: The Journey,* (Springfield, MO: Influence Resources, 2013), 34.
[8] Christopher J. H. Wright, *The Mission of God,* (Downers Grove, IL: InterVarsity Press, 2006), 23.
[9] John Stott, *The Contemporary Christian: An Urgent Plea for Double Listening,* (Downers Grove, IL: InterVarsity Press, 1992), 335.
[10] Alan J. RoxBurgh and M. Scott Boren, *Introducing the Missional Church,* (Grand Rapids, MI: BakerBooks, 2009), Chapter 4, Rethinking the Gospel-the Missio Dei, para. 3.
[11] Wright, *The Mission of God's People,* Chapter 1, God's Purpose, para. 1.
[12] Guinness, *Renaissance,* 87.
[13] Bailey, Chapter 12, Summary: The Inauguration of Jesus' Ministry, para. 4.
[14] Guinness, *Renaissance,* 87.
[15] Barclay, 70.
[16] RoxBurgh and Boren, Introduction, para. 2.
[17] RoxBurgh and Boren, Chapter 3, The Sending of the Church, para. 1.
[18] Ed Stetzer, *Planting Missional Churches,* (Nashville, TN: Broadman & Holman, 2006), 28.
[19] Ibid, 19.
[20] RoxBurgh and Boren, Chapter 2, Mission, para. 1.
[21] Stetzer, 25.
[22] RoxBurgh and Boren, Chapter 5, A Missional Strategy, para. 2.
[23] Alan R. Johnson, *Apostolic Function,* (Pasadena, CA: William Carey Library, 2009), 172.
[24] Ibid, 173.
[25] Stott, *What Christ Thinks of the Church,* 103-104.
[26] Bonhoeffer, 11.

Chapter Nine: Called to Fervor

[1] Stott, *What Christ Thinks of the Church,* 111-112.
[2] Barclay, 83.
[3] Ibid, 85.
[4] Stott, *What Christ Thinks of the Church,* 113.
[5] Ibid, 114.
[6] William Barclay, *The Parables of Jesus,* (Louisville, KY: Westminster John Knox Press, 1970), 125.

[7] Stott, 115.
[8] Stott, *What Christ Thinks of the Church,* 119.
[9] Barclay, *Letters to the Seven Churches,* 83.
[10] Robert Woodberry, "The Missionary Roots of Liberal Democracy," (*American Political Science Review*, May 2012), 39.
[11] John Piper, "Missions: Rescuing from Hell and Renewing the World," (*Desiring God,* January 13th, 2014), http://www.desiringgod.org/articles/missions-rescuing-from-hell-and-renewing-the-world.
[12] Guinness, *Renaissance*, 63.
[13] Stott, *What Christ Thinks of the Church,* 113.
[14] Barclay, *Letters to the Seven Churches,* 87.
[15] Ibid, 88-89.
[16] Ibid, 89.
[17] Stott, *What Christ Thinks of the Church,* 122.
[18] Brogden, 30.
[19] Stanley, 120.
[20] Stott, *What Christ Thinks of the Church*, 118.
[21] Michael J. Gorman, *Reading Revelation Responsibly*, (Eugene, OR: Cascade Books, 2011), 96.
[22] Ibid, 97.
[23] Ibid.
[24] Ibid.

Chapter Ten: Called to Conflict

[1] Eusebius. "The History of the Church," from *Book 7*, (Penguin Books, 1988), 17.
[2] The Israeli Ministry of Tourism has posted signs at the site of Caesarea Philippi detailing these sacrifices and cave reference as the "gates of hell." Primary source documents do not label this cave by this name, but there was a common understanding in the ancient world that water sources served as the entrance to Hades or the underworld below.
[3] Peyton Jones, *Church Zero*, (Colorado Springs, CO: David C Cook, 2013), 222.
[4] C. S. Lewis, *The Four Loves*, (New York, NY: First Mariner Books, 2012), 66.
[5] David Platt, *Radical Together*, (Colorado Springs, CO: Multnomah Books, 2011), 6.
[6] Ferguson, Chapter 6, The Legal Status of Christianity, para. 17.
[7] Guinness, *Renaissance*, 13.
[8] Fatih Cimok, *The Seven Churches*, (Istanbul: A Turizm Yayinlari, 2011), 33-35.

[9] Maddox, 140-141.
[10] Ibid, 141.
[11] Guinness, *Renaissance,* 65.
[12] Ibid, 66.
[13] Brogden, 34.
[14] Ibid, 32.
[15] The Rend Collective Experiment. "Build Your Kingdom Here." From *Campfire* (Integrity Media, 2013).
[16] Bonhoeffer, 27.
[17] Platt, *Radical,* 88.

The Eleventh Chapter: Called to Listen

[1] NLT
[2] Gorman, 99.

Conclusion

[1] These expectations are modifications of a list of family rules a friend, Dick Brogden, shared with me. His family has committed to: love Jesus, not whine, and not quit.

81303325R00140

Made in the USA
Lexington, KY
15 February 2018